Learn
Magic™ Cards

Larry W. Smith, Ph.D.

Wordware Publishing, Inc.

Library of Congress Cataloging-in-Publication Data

Smith, Larry W.
    Learn magic cards / Larry W. Smith.
        p.   cm.
    Includes index.
    ISBN 1-55622-460-5 (pbk.)
    1. Magic: The Gathering (Game)   I. Title.
    GV1469.62.M3S65'   1996
    793.93'2—dc20   95-36554
                                        CIP

ISBN 1-55622-460-5
10 9 8 7 6 5 4 3 2 1
9507

All inquiries for volume purchases of this book should be addressed to Wordware
Publishing, Inc., at the above address. Telephone inquiries may be made by calling:

(214) 423-0090

Contents

Contents

Contents

Acknowledgements

Thanks, Gitty Baxter, for being patient and teaching me how to really play Magic. Much thanks to Jim Furgosi who played many games of Magic with me and gave much of his time in reviewing the manuscript.

Dedication

This book is dedicated to the Smith and Torrez families: Jennifer Smith, Lacey Smith, Jason Smith, my wife, Priscilla Smith, and Eloy & Amelia Torrez, Mike Torrez, David Torrez, Kathleen Bloom, Mary Louise Bermudez, Yolanda Lundsford.

The Lands of Dominia

Fast Effects

Artifacts

Sorceries

Interrupts

Spells

Summon Spells

Enchantments

Artifact Creatures

Instants

Special Abilities

Magic Battlefield

Section 1

About This Book

Introduction

One day, as I was picking up a replacement for a burnt-out condenser for my son's RC-10T race car at a local hobby store, I noticed something unusual in the back of the store—a gathering of some kind. As I walked over to a group of tables pushed together, I observed a number of people of all ages playing some sort of card game. There were stacks of cards everywhere. As I looked over someone's shoulder to get a closer look, I heard a sweet young voice say, "Hey, do you want to play some Magic?"

Somewhat surprised, I replied, "Play what?"

This little girl, who seemed so grown-up, repeated, "Magic—do you want to play a game of Magic?"

Still somewhat bewildered and feeling as if I should know what such a common word should mean, I felt my curiosity rise from a deep sleep. I said, "Yeah, I guess so, but what is Magic? I don't think I have ever heard of it before."

With the patience and composure of an adult and a visible excitement consuming her face, she hurried her words, "Magic is a neat game that you play against someone else. It's cool! It's kind of hard to explain but it's a little like that old game called D&D. It's a lot of fun to play. Do you want to play a game with me?"

What was I to supposed say to this little girl, all of 12 years old? Trying my best not to show my ignorance of yet another term I had not heard of, D&D, I decided to wade in and take a chance. I replied, "OK, I'll give it a try." Boy, what words those turned out to be!

I took my place at one of the tables and proceeded to play my first game of Magic with this enthusiast. Her name was Gitty and I was totally impressed at her mastery of the game; I don't think I need to say who won the contest—your imagination can tell you that!

I had absolutely no idea what a challenging and fascinating world I was entering on that fateful day! And I have never been sorry that I learned to play Magic cards. People of all walks of life and ages play Magic. Thanks, Gitty, for bringing me into the world of Dominia. I will never forget you and I will always consider you my mentor. And to the inventor: Good job! I think you have created a game that will be played by generations to come.

For the First-time Player

Reflecting upon how I got started in Magic, I thought it would be a good idea to write a book aimed at the first-time player. After George Baxter and I finished our first book, *Mastering Magic Cards*, we observed that the person who expresses an interest in learning Magic has no real place to start except to jump right in and play the game. This experience can be quite unpredictable; it can be a humbling experience or it can be disappointing enough not to return to the lands of Dominia. Magic is a complex game. With my second book, *Learn Magic Cards*, the beginner to this great game now has a place to start.

Games and Civilization

Games have fascinated mankind since the beginning of civilized time. As soon as people realized that they had extra time on their hands for something other than survival and hunting, the concept of doing something for fun and reward came into peoples' minds, and games of all kinds were invented. Games are as much a part of us today as is the environment in which we live. Only our imaginations and technology can limit what games we develop in the future. I hope you enjoy the game of Magic and this book.

What Is the Game of Magic?

Magic is a role-playing game played with collectible cards. It is an intellectual battle of *strategy* and *chance* with the simplistic objective of destroying your opponent. Each player attempts to drive the other from the lands of Dominia by playing from a selection of over 1,300 different cards. You can imagine the number of playing combinations that result from this many cards.

In addition to the gaming aspects of Magic, there are other areas of interest such as trading, collecting, magazines, clubs, organizations, comic books, novels, and just getting together with people and having a lot of fun. Magic has brought all of these aspects of the game to the player.

What This Book Will Teach You

Foolish, courageous mortal, you have opted to read yet further and learn how to play the game of Magic. I guess it was just a matter of time. If you feel an uncontrollable need to play, as Gitty so innocently inflicted upon me that first day, then it is best you learn how to play properly and effectively. That is what this book is all about. This book will teach you everything, including terminology, organization of cards, colors of cards, and how to get started playing a game. You will acquire the essential skills to get started playing immediately. After you have played a few games, you will begin to see how comprehensive and fun this game is.

Getting Started and Basic Game Terminology

What Does It Take to Get Started?

After a stimulating duel with Gitty one day, we were wondering what would be the best approach in explaining Magic to a first-time player. Without much hesitation, we both said, "Define some of the most important terms first and then explain how a game is played." This seemed to be a reasonable approach. So be it; this is the course we will embark upon. Before some Magic terminology is introduced, let's see what it takes to get started playing the game.

To get started in Magic, you need the following items:

A. Deck of Magic cards, forty for regular play and sixty for tournaments. Cards can be purchased in Starter Decks of forty or Booster Packs ranging from eight to fifteen cards. It is recommend that you purchase about four to six starter decks and/or booster packs so that you will have a large enough selection of cards to form your first playing deck. You can choose whether you wish to play with forty or sixty cards at this time. It is recommended that you do not play with more than 120 cards total.

If you are a beginner, you should organize your deck of cards into *two* primary *colors* that you want to play with. This will allow you to concentrate on how the game is played without worrying about all the other possibilities that exist. Do not play for "ante" if you are a beginner.

B. Reasonably large flat area to play cards.

C. Device for keeping score: for example, dice (such as a twenty-sided die), counters (normally called "life counters" that can count up to forty life points), or simply pencil and paper.

This is all it takes to begin playing Magic. You should also bring your wit and strategies just in case you might want to win a game or two. We hope your journey into the world of Dominia is a fun and prosperous one.

Types of Magic Cards

There are many different cards in Magic, but they can all be classified into three different categories according to what they do and how they are played:

A. Creatures
B. Lands
C. Spells

Summon "*creature*"	Plains	Enchantments
	Swamps	Sorceries
	Forests	Instants
	Mountains	Interrupts
	Islands	Artifacts

Creature Cards

Within each category are different types of cards. *Creature* cards can be recognized by the words "Summon *creature*," located just below the illustration area, where *creature* is the name of the particular creature. These cards have the ability to attack an opponent and to defend from an attack; this ability is denoted by two numbers separated by a slash in the lower-right hand corner. It is important to note that a creature card is really a "summon spell" until it is placed in the player's territory, and then it becomes a creature. You might say that is has transformed itself from a spell into a creature. The other two numbers, located in the upper right-hand corner of the card, indicate the casting cost that is required to play the card (make this transformation).

Land Cards

Land cards are the most common and frequently used source of *mana*. As a general rule, they do not have any other abilities except to put mana into your pool. After they are played, they remain in the game permanently until destroyed by an opponent's card. Each type of land produces a different color of mana.

Spell Cards

There are six different types of spells: summons, enchantments, sorceries, instants, interrupts and artifacts, and each are played in a slightly different manner. Actually, if you play a card that is not a land card, then you are really casting a spell. And if the spell is successfully played (cast), it is no longer a spell. Some spells are sent to the graveyard after being played and others remain in play, i.e., they are said to be "permanents." Most cards are permanents when in play. These include lands, creatures, artifacts, and enchantments.

Another way of classifying Magic cards is to group them into "mana producing" and "non-mana producing" categories.

New Magic cards are introduced into the game as expansion sets. In case you are interested in which cards come from a particular set, the following is a list of currently available Magic card sets and the order in which they were introduced:

Arabian Nights	First expansion set; identified with the *scimitar* symbol and black borders on the card face. They were recirculated into the Revised edition. This set is based on stories from *The Arabian Nights*. There are approximately ninety-two cards in this set.
Antiquities	Second expansion set; identified with the *anvil* symbol and black borders on the card face. This set is based on *War of the Artificers*. There are approximately 100 cards in this set.
Legends	Third expansion set; identified with a broken column and a gold border.
The Dark	Fourth expansion set; identified with the *crescent* symbol. This set is based on the *Dark Ages of Dominia*.
Fallen Empires	Fifth expansion set; identified with the *crown* symbol and black borders on card face. There are approximately 187 cards.
Ice Age	Sixth expansion set that contains 383 cards and consists of a mixture of lands, artifacts, and cards for all of the colors: gold, white, green, black, red, and blue.
Revised Edition[1]	Standard set; these cards are distributed in Starter Decks and Booster Packs.
Special Promotional Cards[1]	Produced for special events and card sales. Current cards consist of the Nalathni Dragon card (a Summon Dragon with a black border and expansion symbol of a *dragon's head*), which was given to attendees of DragonCon in Atlanta, July 1994, and one card put in *The Duelist* magazine, October 1994, Issue #3, and *Duelist Companion* newsletter, November 1994, Issue #4. The second card is the Sewers of Estark and Arena (a land with a black border and an expansion symbol of a *pen*) and was distributed in the first Magic novel, *Arena*, in September 1994. A third card is the Windseeker Centaur (an instant with a black border and an expansion symbol of a *pen*), which was distributed in the Magic novel *Whispring Woods*.

Limited & *Unlimited* *Only*[1]	The Limited Edition cards are identified by black borders on the card face and consist of two printings, Alpha and Beta, for a total of approximately 302 cards. The Unlimited Edition cards are identified with white borders and later replaced by the Revised Edition. There are approximately thirty-five cards in this set.

[1] Actual Magic: The Gathering sets

As you will discover after playing a few duels, the way in which you play a sequence of cards will vary depending upon the combination of cards previously played. This is one aspect that makes the game of Magic dynamic and unpredictable.

Elements of a Magic Card

Each Magic card contains several elements that identify its type and how it is played. As shown in Figure 2-1, the elements are:

Card Name	The symbolic name of the card.
Cost	The amount of mana and type of mana required to cast the spell.
Type of Spell	The card type which lists the name of the spell that it casts.
Card Text	Description of what action, if any, is to be taken.
Power/Toughness Rating	The amount of power (attack) and toughness (defense) that the card possesses. All creature cards must have a power/toughness rating.
Illustration	The artist's drawing for the card.
Card Illustrator	The name of the artist who created the artwork.
Card Color Area	The border area which indicates the color of the card (red, green, black, white, blue). There are other colors such as brown and beige, but they do not hold any playing significance, and gold, which has to do with multicolor cards.

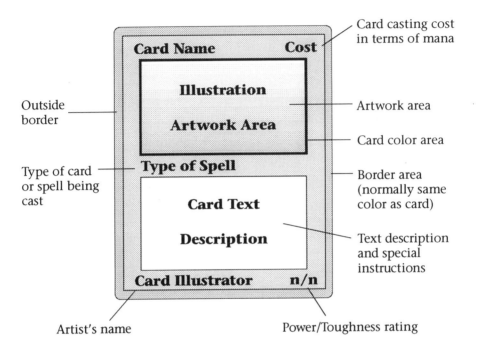

Figure 2-1: Magic Card Layout

Magic Terminology

When you are first starting to play Magic, you need to be aware of certain terms and "magic lingo." This section identifies some of the most common terms and how they are used in playing a game of Magic. With just a little practice, you will be able to master these terms.

Mana and Mana Pool

Mana is one of the most basic and important aspects of Magic. Mana is needed to cast spells or play other cards such as *creatures* so that you can offset your opponent's moves. When you *attack* your opponent, you will need some mana of some kind, in one or more colors, in order to successfully initiate an attack. For example, let's say that you decide to play the *Scryb Sprites* summon card in your hand. To play this card requires one point of *green* mana. This means that you would need to lay down one green mana producing card if you want to play the *Scryb Sprites* card. Some playing cards require more than one mana of the same color or a combination of other color mana cards if you wish to play the particular card. As Gitty reminded me, "If you don't have mana, then you have been reduced to a mere spectator." It's certainly very difficult to play a game of Magic without putting down some sort of mana-producing cards on the playing field.

Mana may be colorless or one of *five* different colors, each with a different set of general capabilities, which can be summarized as follows:

Color	Type of Land[1]	Color Enemies[2]	Typical Usage
White	Plains	Red & Black	Defense
Black	Swamp	White & Green	Creature Attack
Blue	Island	Red & Green	Cast Spells
Red	Mountain	Blue & White	Destroy
Green	Forest	Blue & Black	Heal

Table 2-1: **Mana, Color, and Enemy Table**

[1] There are other cards that can produce mana besides land cards.

[2] The term *enemies* refers to the weakness that a particular color has with respect to others. For example, the colors red and black have stronger characteristics over the color white.

The above table can be used to categorize the various color choices and how they can be used in specific instances. The color of the mana is linked to the color of a specific card. The most common source of mana are *land* cards, but there are a wide variety of other cards that can also produce mana. One such land card is a mountain which says to "add one red mana to your mana pool." The *Dark Ritual* card, another source for mana that is not a land card, is an interrupt and says to "add three black mana to your mana pool."

If you are a first-time player, don't be fooled at the apparent simplicity of mana; there are a number of different ways to produce mana in a game. Besides playing land cards to produce mana, you can play other card types which also put mana into your mana pool.

Colors

As described in the mana section, each card that you play in Magic has a specific color: *white, black, blue, red,* or *green.* The color is shown in the inside border located in the upper-half of the card (see Figure 2-1) and is important when you play cards that require a specific color of mana. One reason for having five different colors is so that you can group cards into five different categories to give the game more variation, thus making it more difficult for your opponent to predict what type of deck you might construct. As mentioned earlier, the first-time player should select only two colors of playing cards and should organize the deck to have at least twenty mana producing cards (lands), twenty creature cards, and the rest other card types such as spells. This will give you a good starting deck to play and provide the best chance of being able to play your cards the most effective way. After you become an advanced player, you will be able to construct decks that work best for how you play the game.

Tapping

Tapping is one of the most fundamental game actions and tells your opponent that you have played a spell. Tapping is used in two different situations. First, during game play, turning a card sideways, ninety degrees or less, is called *tapping* (see Figure 2-2) and is done to show that the card (or cards) have been used or played. For example, if I have an Island land card that I have previously put into play and I decide to bring a creature card into play, say the *Merfolk of the Pearl Trident*, a Summon Merfolk card, I would play this card next to the Island. You normally do this by putting the creature card on top of the land card then turn them both sideways (Figure 2-2). Once the *Merfolk of the Pearl Trident* card is tapped, it cannot attack or defend from an attack until it has been untapped. Although the land card is also tapped, you don't have to be concerned about it because it is not a creature card and cannot attack.

The other aspect of tapping is the *tap symbol*, which is usually the first item in the text portion of the card. The tap symbol is either the letter **T** circled and slanted at an angle or a square with a curved arrow on it; both are followed by a colon.

When a card has this symbol, it must be *tapped* whenever its power or ability is used, i.e., whenever it is played as described above with the *Merfolk of the Pearl Trident* card. This means that the card cannot be used again until it is untapped, either in the Untap phase or by the actions of other cards. Some of the more common cards that have this symbol are land cards, as shown in Table 2-1.

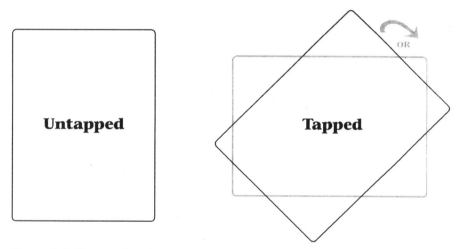

Figure 2-2: Untapped and Tapped Card Positions

Although we have not yet discussed the various game phases, this card is played in your *Main* phase after the first three phases, *Untap*, *Upkeep*, and *Draw*, have been played.

Untapping

The reverse action of *tapping* is *untapping*. When it is your turn to play, the very first thing you *must* do is to *untap* (turn upright) all of your cards that are tapped. This occurs in the very first turn phase called the Untap phase. This has the effect of resetting the playing field and putting your cards in an initial (unplayed) state so they can later be used. When you are in the process of untapping your cards, your opponent cannot play any cards such as spells or fast effects until you have finished. There is only one exception to this rule, and that is if a card specifically prevents you from doing so in the text portion of the card. It is very common to untap several cards once you get into a game.

Casting a Spell

This is one of the most basic moves a player makes in Magic. When you cast a spell against your opponent, you are putting a creature card (as opposed to a land card) into play and you are considered to be the *controller* of that card at that point in time. You know that you are casting a spell because you are not playing a land card; you are playing cards that are *summons, enchantments, sorceries, instants, interrupts,* and *artifacts.* A spell that is not an instant or interrupt must be played in the Main phase. Don't forget that when you cast a spell, it is discarded and put into the graveyard after being played.

You might note a spell is only a spell while it is in your hand. Once you play the card, it then becomes a creature, artifact, enchantment, etc.

Attacking

After you have finally placed at least *one creature* card in play, you may initiate attacks. This is done in the *Main* phase only, and you must announce to your opponent that you are attacking so he or she can begin preparing a proper defense. You must be aware that once you have announced you are attacking, your opponent can respond with cards that have spells or special abilities that specify "...before the attack" in the text portion of the card. After these have been played and resolved, you can then initiate your attack with as many creature cards that you control as you wish. Don't forget to tap each creature that you are attacking with, and do not use cards in play that are already tapped to attack. After you have chosen your attacking cards, then you and your opponent can play any fast effects if desired.

It is courteous for you to announce your attack first by saying "I'm attacking" before you tap your cards. This is because you are obligated to give your opponent a chance to use any fast effects to cast spells or use special abilities before attacking cards that are tapped. You might also note that you squander (eliminate) the attack phase by announcing that you are attacking with no creatures. This prevents your opponent from using spells or special abilities that could be cast before you initiate your attack.

Defending

After you initiate an attack, your opponent has the option of choosing which creatures are to put up a defense against the attack. For each creature you are attacking with, your opponent must decide how many creatures, if any, will block. You cannot block two or more attacking creatures with one defending creature, but more than one defending creature may block a single attacking creature. Don't forget that a creature that is tapped cannot defend.

Casting Cost

It will cost you points if you want to cast a spell on your opponent and inflict some damage. When you play a card that casts a spell, you must spend points of mana from your available mana pool. The casting cost is shown in the upper right-hand corner of a card by two types of symbols: mana symbol and number.

Mana that is represented by the symbol of its color (red, black, blue, green, white) indicates how many points of mana of that particular color is required to cast the spell. If the number is in a gray circle, then you must choose additional mana of any color that you have in play. For example, if I want to cast the *Pearled Unicorn,* which is a Summon Unicorn card, I would need one point of white mana and two points of other mana in order to play it. If I had one white plains card and two other blue islands in play, then I could play this card by tapping it and the two other land cards. If this play is successful, I now have a creature card with a power/toughness of 2/2 that I can use to attack my opponent's cards.

The Library

The library is your reservoir of playing cards. The library consists of a deck of carefully selected cards, a minimum of forty for dueling and sixty for tournaments, that a player draws from during his or her turn. This deck is shuffled and then placed face down in front of the player. In games that are unstructured, the deck does not have to be shuffled and the number of cards can vary. A player must always attempt to draw **one** card from the top of the library during the *Main* phase. If a player is unable to draw a card from the library, then the contest is lost. You might also be aware that some cards have the special ability to cause the library to be reshuffled and perform other actions during the game such as swapping the top card, moving cards from the graveyard to the library, reshuffling graveyard into library, discarding cards from the library, shuffling players' hands into the library, etc.

Graveyard

The graveyard consists of cards that have been *destroyed* during the course of play for various reasons. Each player has his own grave-yard of cards that have been destroyed. A card can be sent to the graveyard when a spell or effect takes it out of play, thereby preventing it from being used either temporarily or for the entire game. It should be noted that some cards have undergone wording changes in the text portion of the card. For example, the word *discarded* should be replaced with *destroyed* for cards such as *Balance, Bottle of Suleiman, Black Lotus, Chaos Orb, City in a Bottle, Conversion, Cyclone, Disenchant, Drop of Honey, Jihad, Pestilence, Tranquility*, and *Unsummon*.

Buried, Killed, Destroyed

Your shovel, if it were legal in Magic, might come in handy here. When a card is buried (destroyed or killed), it is sent to the grave-yard, but it might only be a temporary stay. It can be put back into play (if it was not buried) if another card has the special ability of regeneration and regenerates it back into play.

Regeneration

A card can be regenerated and put back into play if another card allows it to be or if the card itself has its own built-in regeneration ability. If a card is regenerated, it comes back in tapped mode. It is important to note that a card can only be regenerated during the turn in which it was sent to the graveyard. You cannot regenerate a card that was sent to the graveyard in a previous turn.

Removed

Your shovel or any other device is ineffective when a card is removed from the land of Dominia. When a card is removed, it is taken out of the game and placed in a separate pile other than your graveyard. These cards must remain in this pile and cannot be shuffled back into the graveyard during the game.

Power and Toughness

Cause and effect have their unique role to play in Magic. Power and toughness are the forces of *offense* and *defense* that a creature possesses. When you initiate an attack on your opponent or your opponent initiates an attack on you, the *power* and *toughness* values on a card, located in the lower right corner of the card denoted by n/n, are brought into play and used to attack and defend the card. When you attack, you *attack* or *inflict damage* equivalent to the power rating specified on the card, and your opponent must defend with the toughness rating on the card being attacked. If the power value of the attacking card is greater than or equal to the toughness value on the card that is being attacked, the target dies and is sent to the graveyard. Otherwise, the target blocks (survives) the attack and absorbs the damage *cumulatively* during the entire game. Cumulatively means that if the same card is attacked more than once, all damage is totaled and applied against the toughness value. Any accumulated damage is healed (removed) during the *Heal Creatures* phase. If a creature's toughness value falls below 1 at any time, it is dead and sent to the graveyard. And if a creature's power falls below 1 (and it is common for it to be negative), it will be unable to deal any damage when it attacks. As you can see, power and toughness are just two of many common sources of a creature's special ability.

Blocking

When a creature is attacked by another creature, it either survives the attack or dies and is sent to the graveyard. If the power rating on the attacking creature is less than the toughness rating on the target creature under attack, then the creature under attack has successfully *blocked* the attack. The toughness rating on the target creature being attacked is reduced by the number of points specified on the attacking card's power rating. Otherwise, it dies. If a card is tapped, then it cannot block.

An important point to remember is that a player can choose not to block an attack from his or her opponent. Although this is not a common action, the player being attacked loses a total number of life points corresponding to the attacker's power rating. An example of this would be a situation in which the card under attack is so valuable that it is better to absorb life points and keep it in play than sacrifice the card or lower its defense capabilities.

Life Counter

A life counter is one of several devices used to keep track of life points. You can just as well use a twenty-sided die or keep score on a piece of paper or a calculator.

Territory

Each player has his or her own playing area called the *territory*. This is where you and your opponent play your cards. See Figure 2-3, which shows the complete Magic playing field and where each player's territory is located. This is also called the lands of Dominia.

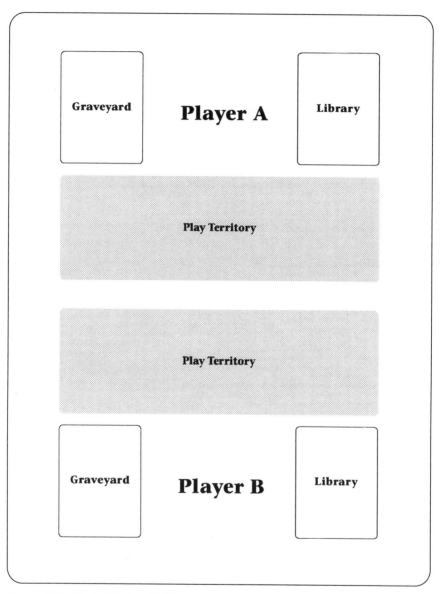

Figure 2-3: Magic Playing Field

Turn Phases

Untap The Untap phase (first phase) of a game of Magic is where any tapped cards are untapped, i.e., turned to their upright position (see Figure 2-2).

Upkeep During the Upkeep phase (second phase), a player must pay mana and/or sacrifice cards in order to avoid other actions such as losing life points. That is, some cards require you to take certain actions, as stated in the text portion of the card, during this phase. You could think of this as a maintenance phase where actions are reset before further play is continued.

Draw The third phase requires that you draw one card from the top of your library. If you are unable to draw a card, then you have lost the duel.

Main Phase This is the fourth phase; its purpose is to allow you to put a land card into play to increase your mana pool, initiate an attack on your opponent, or cast any spells. Any or all of these actions can be done in any order, but only once per turn.

Discard In the fifth phase, the Discard phase, you must examine your playing hand and discard (send to the graveyard) any cards beyond a total of seven. You may have fewer than seven cards but no more than seven. Discarded cards must be placed face-up because the graveyard is always a potential source of cards that could become active at a later point in the game. You must let your opponent see what has been sent to the graveyard.

Inform Opponent In the Inform Opponent phase (sixth phase) you tell your opponent that you are finished with your turn. Since the Main phase has no set order of actions, this phase is used to let your opponent know that you have completed that phase, and hence, your turn.

Heal Creatures There comes a time in any battle to lick your wounds and remove the dead from the battlefield. The Heal Creatures phase is the last phase of a game of Magic where the purpose is to heal (erase) all damage that was done in the previous game phases to creatures before your opponent's turn begins. The overall purpose of this phase is to bring the game to a known state before play resumes.

Permanent

Some card types are heroic and tough enough to stay around for the entire battle, irregardless of the outcome. Any card that is a land, creature, artifact, or enchantment will remain in play continuously (the entire game) until it is either destroyed or removed from the game by one of your opponent's cards. Hence, the name *permanent* is given to these types of cards. Other types of cards are automatically discarded when they have been played, such as instants, sorceries, and interrupts. Examples of permanent cards are lands, artifacts, creatures, and enchantments, and they automatically become permanents as soon as they are put into play. For example, the *Mountain* and *Forest* are both land cards and are permanent when successfully played. The *Earthbind* is an Enchant Creature card that remains in play permanently once it has been played.

Continuous

How is it possible to play a game of poker without ante and remain in the game? Well, this is the story of a card that is *continuous*; it and any effects it may have can be played continuously (each turn) during the entire duel. We will discuss a card's *effects* later. Continuous cards are those that have no casting cost. For example, the *Ornithopter* is an Artifact Creature card that has a casting cost of zero and therefore becomes a continuous card once it has been cast. But, don't forget, a land card is also a continuous card because it has no casting cost.

Fast Effects

Being too eager can be a virtue in Magic! A card with fast effects can be played in any phase of the game at any point in time except in the Heal Creatures phase. This is what makes a fast effects card extremely useful. Fast effects cards are interrupts, instants and abilities of permanents that are not continuous. Special abilities are described in the text part of the card. For example, the *Dark Ritual* card is an interrupt with the special ability to "add three black mana to your mana pool," and the *Blue Elemental Blast* is an interrupt with the special ability to "counter a red spell that is being cast or destroy a red card in play."

Fast effects are called that because they can start before another spell has had a chance to finish.

Special Abilities

Some cards, for no apparent reason, are born with abilities beyond the normal mortal. This can really be annoying at times for opposing creatures! Special abilities refer to a card that possesses one or more actions beyond that of a normal creature card. These abilities are described in the text part of the card. For example, some of these special abilities are banding, flying, first strike, protection, trample, rampage, and walking. In order to play these abilities, you might have to spend some mana or tap one of your creatures in play. Examples of cards that contain special abilities are the *Samite Healer*, which is a *Summon Cleric* card that says it "prevents one damage to any target card," and the *Conversion*, an enchantment card with special ability to "convert all mountains to basic plains as long as Conversion is in play." Another card that has a life-giving special ability is the *Soul Net*, which is an artifact card that says "you gain one life point each time a creature is sent to the graveyard." This means that each time a card from your or your opponent's hand is sent to the graveyard, you gain one life point. This could be a very good card to put in any deck!

Sacrificing

Life is full of sacrifices, but nothing like in the game of Magic! A card is sacrificed and sent to the graveyard when the text portion of the card states that this must happen. For example, the *Strip Mine* and *Armor Thrulls* are two cards that sacrifice themselves after being played. The card is considered to be buried and cannot be regenerated and brought back into play. A player cannot sacrifice a card that is under the control of another player or one that has received a lethal (deadly) amount of damage. If a card is already on its way to the graveyard, then you also cannot sacrifice the card. For example, *Tormod's Crypt* is an artifact card that says to "sacrifice this card if you wish to remove all cards in target player's graveyard from the game."

Target

In battle, everyone is a potential target at all times! The term *target* simply refers to any card in play you may want to target and cast a spell against. The term target can also used to refer to an individual player or token. This could be your card or your opponent's card. You might note that some spells do not require a target card to cast while others require more than one target.

This term can be confusing at times. For example, the *Psychic Venom* card takes one point of damage whenever the land is tapped. The text on this card says "when target land is tapped" which means whenever your or your opponent's lands are tapped.

One very important rule in Magic is that you cannot cast a spell unless there is at least one creature card in play (i.e., a viable target). For example, if I decide to play the *Psychic Venom* card, which is an Enchant Land, the spell is cast if the text part of the card states that "when a target land becomes tapped, two points of damage is dealt to target land's controller." Or another very effective card is the *Lifetap*, which is an Enchantment which says that "you gain one life point each time a forest card of your opponent's is tapped." This means that each time he tries to play a card that requires green mana, you gain one life point for each forest tapped to cast it.

You should also be aware that some of the earlier cards do not use the word "target" directly in the text portion of the card. A spell or effect is said to be "targeted" (can specify any card or player) if the player has any choice in what it affects. Otherwise, it is not targeted. In these cases, a target is implied such as with the *Simulacrum* card which is an instant and the *Volcanic Eruption* card which is a sorcery. The *Wrath of God* card which is a sorcery and the *Thicket Basilisk* which is a summon Basilisk are not targeted.

Tokens

A token is simply a marker or some other type of object that is used to represent a card that you must play but do not have with you in your hand or library. Some cards have a spell that forces you to put a specific type of card in play and a token is used to represent that card as if it were actually present. It is important to note that spells which would normally affect non-token cards in play do not affect tokens themselves. *Wrath of God* kills all token creatures.

Owner, Caster

Each player is always the *owner* of his or her cards. This never changes during the course of a duel except for a handful of special ante spells. If you are not playing for ante, then these special spells do not apply. Whenever you play a card, you are always considered to be the *caster*. So, the owner and caster of a card are always the same person.

Controller

The controller of a card refers to the player who is currently in control of the card. When you first play a card, you are the controller of the card. Your opponent can cast a spell that reverses control of a card such that it is now the other player's card to play. When a card refers to "you" it means the player who controls the card; when the word "your" is used, this means the card that you control, irrespective of who actually owns it. If a card has been protected by a special ability of another card, then control cannot be taken away.

Artifact

An *artifact* is one of the most basic types of spells that can be cast in Magic. This type of spell can only be cast during the Main phase of the game. If the artifact is required to be tapped, then it cannot be used again until it is untapped. Also, if the artifact does not have a tap symbol (letter T slanted in the text part of the card) or have a cost to use, then it is considered to be continuous and its effects (if any) are active until it is untapped. An artifact can be countered by an interrupt, and once an artifact has been successfully cast, it can only be affected by other spells that affect artifacts. An example of an artifact card is the *Obsianus Golem* that has no special abilities and is played as an artifact with a power/toughness rating of 6/6. Another example of an artifact that is more powerful in what it can do is the *Ivory Cup*, which states "give one life point when any white spell is cast." One of my favorite artifacts is *Aladdin's Lamp*, which allows you to "draw X cards in your Main phase and keep only one card." This is a great card, as it allows you to select any card from your X cards drawn with the *Lamp*.

Other More Advanced Terms

The following are terms that you will encounter after playing Magic for a while. They are defined here for your convenience and reference.

Interrupts and Timing

If lightning from the heavens interrupts your battle, then it is time to yield to this insurmountable force. The term *interrupt* refers to a type of spell that can be played *immediately* during your or your opponent's turn. You might view this as interrupting your opponent's spell, and it is the only way that a fast effect can be countered. Once the effect is played, it must be sent to the graveyard. Its effects on other spells are permanent. You and your opponent can play as many interrupts as desired and even interrupt your own spells if desired. Interrupts are considered to be a type of fast effect. An example of an interrupt card is the *Spell Blast*, which says to "counter target spell and make X the casting cost of the target spell" or the *Mana Drain*, which says "counters target spell being cast and give you X colorless mana next turn where X is the cost of the spell countered."

After you have played an interrupt, you can interrupt the interrupt card you just played. This is called *timing*. If both players want to play spells at the same time, the person whose turn it is goes first.

Banding

There is strength in numbers. Banding is a creature's special ability that allows it to combine with other creature cards in order to form a more formidable force while attacking. Banding can only be done in the Attack phase and has the added advantage of allowing the player to control where the damage is distributed. Once these cards are formed into a single band, they are considered to be a group when attacking and defending. When attacking, all cards in the band must be blocked together or otherwise allowed through. Similarly, when defending, any number of cards can join together to block another attacker. The banding ability was first introduced in the Legends set and can be used as a very effective means for attacking and defending. The card that is banded does not inherit any special abilities. If you attack with two creatures that are banded together, then you choose which target creature under attack dies (if any). Also, if you attack two creatures that are bonded, then your opponent chooses which creature dies (if any).

Trample

Trample is a card's special ability that allows any *excess* damage inflicted on an attacking creature to be directly applied to the defending player. Trample damage only applies to an attacking creature that has this special ability, and if this is blocked by one or more defending creatures, the attacker chooses how to assign the damage to one or more of the defending creatures. Any excess damage that cannot be assigned is passed along to the player. You might also note that the defending creature could have protection from trample as a special ability, and in such a case, the player will not suffer any damage.

Flying

Some special abilities in Magic simply give a creature an additional ability that can only be countered by another card with the same ability. A creature that has flying ability cannot be blocked by a non-flying creature. For example, *Serra Angel* is a Summon Angel card that has the flying ability. *Mesa Pegasus* is a Summon Pegasus card that has both flying and banding special abilities. Another example is *Flight*, which is an Enchant Creature card that states "a target creature becomes a flying creature."

Landwalk

Like the flying ability, the landwalk is an example of another type of special ability called "evasion ability" that is given to *swampwalk, mountainwalk, islandwalk*, etc. cards. This card prevents a card with *landtype* walk ability from being blocked if the defender has any land cards with the *landtype* ability. For example, *Devouring Deep* is a Summon Devouring Deep card that has islandwalk ability. *Lord of Atlantis* is a Summon Lord card with islandwalk ability. *Lost Soul* is a Summon Lost Soul card with swampwalk ability.

First Strike

First strike is a special ability that allows a creature to inflict its damage first before another creature. This occurs in the Attack part of the Main phase and all creatures, whether they be yours or your opponent's, with first strike capability deal their damage at the same time. There is only one level of first strike capability. For example, *Kobold Overlord* is a Summon Lord card with first strike ability. *Lance* is an Enchant Creature card with first strike ability. And *Rapid Fire* is an instant with first strike ability. The key to interpreting first strike is that the card that has this capability is played before cards without first strike capability. This can be particularly damaging to an attacking player who does not have any cards with first strike capability, as his opponent could inflict some damage if he has first strike ability.

Protection

Some creatures have the ability to be protected against certain colors. If damage is dealt to a creature with protection, it is reduced to zero and the creature cannot be blocked by creatures of the same color. In addition, the creature with protection cannot be targeted by a spell or effect of the same color. On the other hand, it can be affected by spells or effects of the same color that do not specifically target it. There are couple of additional rules associated with protection from color:

1. If there are any color enchantments already on a creature, they are dismissed.

2. Since the damage is targeted and not the creature, damage can be presented by color spells and effects.

For example, *Beasts of Bogardan* is a Summon Beasts card with protection ability. *Black Ward* is an Enchant Creature card which has protection from the color black. And *Knights of Thorn* is a Summon Knights card which has protection from the color green.

Walls

A wall is a special type of creature that is not allowed to initiate an attack, even if the power rating is greater than zero. It could do damage while defending. Enchant spells can be cast on them since they are creatures. Other than that restriction, this type of creature acts the same as all other normal creatures. A wall can also be tapped. For example, *Wall of Stone* is a Summon Stone card that has wall blocking ability. *Wall of Wonder* is a Summon Wall card with wall blocking ability in addition to other abilities. And *Wall of Spears* is an Artifact Creature card with both wall and first strike abilities. In summary, walls are simply creatures that cannot attack.

Sacrifice

Some cards have powerful abilities and require that something else be sacrificed in order to complete the spell. All spells in Magic have two parts when they are cast: a *cost* (usually some mana) and a *result* (what happens when the spell is fully resolved). A sacrifice is essentially a cost that cannot be prevented; it must be played and then sent to the graveyard. You can sacrifice any card that you control. For example, if you have two *Farmsteads* in play and wish to gain life from both of them, you must pay four white mana, two for each *Farmstead*. Some cards sacrifice themselves after being used, such as the *Strip Mine* and *Armor Thrulls*. Remember, sorceries are sent directly to the graveyard after they've been cast. Many of the cards that require a sacrifice are either black or artifacts.

Section 3

The Playing Field

The Lands Of Dominia

When you battle your opponent in a game of Magic, you are playing on an imaginary plane or field called *Dominia*. This playing area is similar to a chess or Monopoly board. Wherever you play a game of Magic, the playing field is where you duel against your opponent.

Playing Field Layout

The playing field consists of three basic parts:

1. *Library* for each player—stack of cards to draw from.
2. *Playing territory* for each player—put cards into play.
3. *Graveyard* for each player—cards that have been buried (killed).

Figure 3-1 shows the typical playing field for a two-person game. Each player has his own library, graveyard, and playing territory with an imaginary line drawn between them.

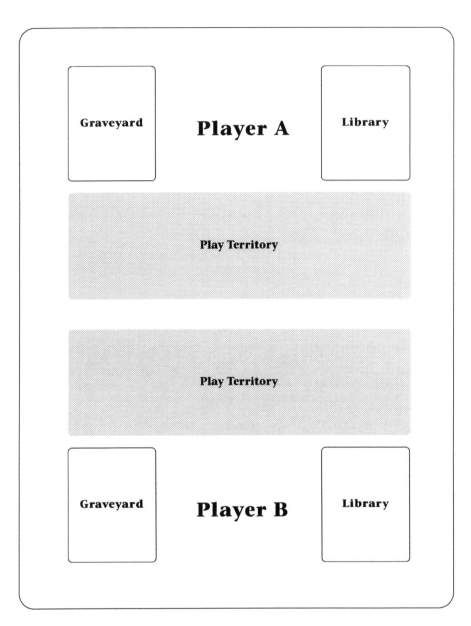

Figure 3-1: Magic Playing Field

Library

Not to be confused with the Library of Alexandria, the *library* is your reservoir of playing cards. It is the pile of cards that you draw from during your turn. The deck must be shuffled and placed face down in front of each player before the contest begins. Be aware that your opponent can play a card that will force you to draw one or more cards from your library or perform some other desirable or undesirable action such as reshuffling the library. For example, *Demonic Tutor* is a sorcery card that says to "take any one card from your library and reshuffle it afterwards." Generally speaking, this can be a very desirable thing to do, especially if you are able to better select a card that can benefit you. Remember, your opponent can defeat you if you are unable to draw from your library!

Graveyard

Not to dwell in the macabre, but there is a dead zone in Dominia where cards go when they have been taken out of action and their memories erased. When a card is *destroyed*, *buried*, or *removed* from the game during combat, it is sent to the graveyard. Each player has a graveyard of cards. A creature can avoid being sent to the graveyard by the action of another card by playing a special ability or a spell. If it is successful in returning to play, it is undamaged and must be tapped. The following applies to cards sent to the graveyard:

> Cards that are *buried* or *removed* cannot be regenerated.
> Cards that are *killed* or *destroyed* can be regenerated.

Some cards may change the above rules as denoted in the text portion of the card. Another important aspect of cards in the graveyard is that they have no memory as to how they arrived there and how they have been previously played.

Playing Territory

The playing territory or playing field is the area in front of both players where cards are played and the actual duel takes place. All seven phases of the game (Untap, Upkeep, Draw, Main, Discard, Inform, and Heal) are played out in this area. To play a card, you place it face-up in either an untapped or tapped position. For example, if you are playing a land card in your Main phase, it is placed in a untapped position. If you are playing a creature card, then it is placed in a tapped position along with the cards that are required to play it.

The Sideboard

The sideboard should be located somewhere outside the playing field (Figure 3-1) so these cards do not get confused with other cards in play. Although the sideboard is an optional part of a game, it can be used very effectively in playing and deck construction. As you finish each game, you can keep a separate file of fifteen to twenty cards that can be exchanged with cards in your playing deck at the start of each new game. This can only be done at the end of the game; cards from the sideboard cannot be brought into play during the duel. The real purpose of the sideboard is to allow a player to make adjustments to his or her playing deck according to how the duel is progressing.

Section 4

Playing the Colors

The Colors of Magic

As discussed in an earlier section, points of *mana* are needed to cast any spells or play other cards such as creatures so that you can use them later to initiate attacks on your opponent. When you attack your opponent, you need to have one or more creature cards in play, which means you already must have the proper number of mana cards of some color in play. These cards are normally land cards. You can tell the color of a card by the thin inside border area that surrounds the artwork. The color on some cards is hard to distinguish, but you should always be able to recognize it by its mana symbol. Mana can be colorless or one of *five* different colors and come from two types of sources:

A. The five basic land cards:

Plains	*White* mana	(enemies are red and black)
Swamps	*Black* mana	(enemies are white and green)
Islands	*Blue* mana	(enemies are red and green)
Mountains	*Red* mana	(enemies are blue and white)
Forests	*Green* mana	(enemies are blue and black)

B. Other cards that specify which type of mana to play (described in the text portion of the card). Some examples are *Badlands, Basalt Monolith, Birds of Paradise, Celestral Prism, Dark Ritual, Elves of Deep Shadow, Fellwar Stone, Llanowar Elves, Mana Flare, Mox Ruby*[1], *Mox Pearl*[1],

Mox Sapphire[1], Mox Jet[1], Plateau, Princess Lucrezia, Riven Turnbull, Savannah, Scrubland, Sol Ring, etc.

[1] These cards are restricted in tournament play.

The colorless mana cards may be brown or beige and are artifact, artifact-creature, and other lands cards and are used to produce mana and cast spells. Sometimes it is hard to visually distinguish them from other cards.

When you first construct your playing deck, we recommend that you pick only two colors and build your deck around those colors. Choosing a particular color for the first time is a little difficult since you have not had a chance to play much. Gitty's favorite color is blue because it brings out a mischievous side of her personality. My favorite colors are a combination of blue and white because they are very effective at casting spells and provide an adequate means of defense. If your objective is to have a very effective attack game yet be able to heal your creatures, then you should choose black and green. By choosing only two colors when you first play, you will be able to focus on the basic aspects of the game and still be able to play a respectable game. As you become more experienced, you will discover various other techniques for constructing your decks that could include a mixture of other colors.

You might also want to refer to *Mastering Magic Cards*, also from Wordware Publishing, which goes into the art of masterful deck construction and overall playing techniques. This book also shows you how to tie elements of fundamental decks to more advanced concept cards and how to create effective tournament decks with minimal investment. The book also teaches sound strategy through creativity and intelligent game play—the essentials of superior Magic play!

Now is the appropriate time to describe how to play cards of different colors. In order to explain the differences in each color, we will use actual cards to illustrate their strengths and weaknesses and how they can be played. You might note that there are over 1,300 Magic cards in existence today, so we will only discuss a select few. Appendix H contains a list of all cards in the Revised edition.

White: Protection

The color *white* encompasses cards that are more defense oriented than cards of other colors. These cards are strong in the healing and protection areas and have the ability to remove nearly any offensive opposing card.

Color:	*White*
Name:	*Conversion*
Type:	*Enchantment*
Casting Cost:	*2WW*
Power/ Toughness:	---

Text

Convert all mountains to basic plains during conversion. Pay WW during upkeep or card is destroyed.

Color:	*White*
Name:	*Healing Salve*
Type:	*Instant*
Casting Cost:	*W*
Power/ Toughness:	---

Text

Gain 3 life points, or prevent up to 3 damage if dealt from a single target.

Figure 4-1: *Conversion*, Enchantment   Figure 4-2: *Healing Salve*, Instant

The cards above are examples of two white cards that are played in different ways. First, *Conversion* is an enchantment card that requires two white mana and two other color mana to play (cast). The casting cost is shown in the upper-right corner of the card. The notation "2WW" on the above card means "two mana of any color and two white mana." On the actual card itself, the 2 is placed inside a circle and the WW is replaced with two white mana symbols. You should be aware that there can be any combination of numbers and letters that represent the total mana required to cast a particular card. For example, 1WWW means "one other color mana and three white mana." When the *Conversion* card is successfully cast, it forces your opponent to convert all cards that are mountains (if any) to plains. This is a good card to play, because if you are playing the color white (plains) and your opponent is playing some other color such as red (mountains), this card can change all his or her mana from red to white, thereby significantly reducing the possibility of being able to cast creature spells. This assumes, of course, that there are no other cards in play that are not mountains that have mana. The only problem with playing this card is that it requires two points of white mana each turn in order to stay in play. This is called its "upkeep" cost and is played in the Upkeep phase. You must decide if you can afford two white mana to keep this card in play or if you should use the mana for some other spell or ability.

The second card, *Healing Salve*, is an instant that only requires one white mana to cast. This card offers you a choice of playing one of two different actions: gain three life points or prevent three points of damage from occurring to a single target. Depending upon the game situation, you may choose one option over the other. If you are low on life points, then you might want to choose the first option and gain an additional three life points. Or you may choose to prevent up to three points of damage from being dealt to you when a single target card is attacked.

White has a slow development time and often requires several cards together to be totally effective. Other effective white cards are *Benalish Hero*, *Mesa Pegasus*, *War Elephant*, *Tundra Wolf*, *Pikeman*, and *Serra Angel*.

Black: Death

The color black contains cards that provide a greater level of attack capabilities than cards of other colors. These cards are strong in destroying your opponent. There are powerful enchantments such as *Pestilence* and *The Abyss*. Black has the greatest power for destruction of lands.

Color:	*Black*
Name:	*Terror*
Type:	*Instant*
Casting Cost:	*1B*
Power/ Toughness:	---

Text

Bury a target creature. This card cannot target black creatures or artifact creatures.

Color:	*Black*
Name:	*Frozen Shade*
Type:	*Summon Shade*
Casting Cost:	*2B*
Power/ Toughness:	*2/2*

Text

Upkeep B: +1/+1

Figure 4-3: *Terror*, Instant

Figure 4-4: *Frozen Shade*, Summon Shade

The first card, *Terror*, is an instant that requires one black mana and one other color mana to cast. When successfully cast, it buries (sends to the graveyard) any target creature, namely one of your opponent's. The only restriction is that you cannot choose a target creature that is either black or an artifact creature. Remember, your opponent can regenerate this card before the end of your turn if he or she has the appropriate special ability or card to do so.

The second card, *Frozen Shade*, a Summon Shade card which requires one black mana and two other color mana to cast, can attack your opponent with a power of 2 and toughness of 2 and adds +1/+1 (power/toughness) to all black creature cards in play. This ability is called "pumping," and the attacking card is called a "pumpable" card. This is a fairly powerful card because it strengthens the overall attack (power) and defense (toughness) capabilities of all black creatures in play. Note that this card has an *upkeep* cost of one black mana to stay in play. The upkeep cost is indicated by the text preceding the ":" in the text description area of the card.

Black has practically no defense against other enchantments and artifacts such as *Cleanse* and *Karma*. Also, black has very few methods of regaining life points. Some other powerful black cards are *Yogmoth Demon* and *Lord of the Pit*.

Blue: Counter Magic

The color blue is one of the most effective colors of the game and encompasses cards that provide a more powerful means for casting spells than other colors. These cards can deceive your opponent into thinking that their abilities are not powerful. Blue's counterspell abilities are also very strong.

Color:	*Blue*
Name:	*Feedback*
Type:	*Enchant Enchantment*
Casting Cost:	*2U*
Power/ Toughness:	---

Text

One damage to controller of target enchantment during controller's upkeep.

Color:	*Blue*
Name:	*Flight*
Type:	*Enchant Creature*
Casting Cost:	*U*
Power/ Toughness:	---

Text

Make any target creature a flying creature.

Figure 4-5: *Feedback*, Enchant Enchantment

Figure 4-6: *Flight*, Enchant Creature

The first card, *Feedback*, is an enchant enchantment card that costs one blue mana and two other color mana to cast. This card inflicts one point of damage to the person who controls any target enchantment card that you choose and must be played during the upkeep phase only.

The second card, *Flight*, is an enchant creature card that costs only one blue mana to cast. Once successfully cast, you can choose any target creature that you have in play to receive the "flying" ability, a creature with a special ability that means it can only be blocked by another card that also has the same ability. In addition, flying creatures can block other non-flying creatures. If you do not have any creature cards in play and still wish to play this card, then you must select one of your opponent's creature cards to receive the flying ability. This, however, would probably be an undesirable move to make, but it shows how flexible the game of Magic can be.

Blue has the unique ability to copy and steal artifacts and creatures. But blue is lacking in its ability to deal with artifacts and enchantments in general. Some powerful blue cards are *Counterspell*, *Power Sink*, and *Mana Drain*.

Red: Destruction

The color red includes cards that provide a more complete set of destructive capabilities than cards of other colors. These cards are strong in the total destructive area of dealing powerful spells.

Color:	*Red*
Name:	*Gray Ogre*
Type:	*Summon Ogre*
Casting Cost:	*2R*
Power/ Toughness:	*2/2*

Text

Color:	*Red*
Name:	*Disintegrate*
Type:	*Sorcery*
Casting Cost:	*XR*
Power/ Toughness:	---

Text

Do X damage to any target. If target dies this turn, it is removed entirely from the game. Cannot regenerate this turn.

Figure 4-7: *Gray Ogre*, Summon Ogre   Figure 4-8: *Disintegrate*, Sorcery

The first card, *Gray Ogre*, is a Summon Ogre card which costs one red mana and two other color mana to cast. This card has no special abilities and can only be used to attack an opponent's card with a power of 2. It also has a defense of 2.

The second card, *Disintegrate*, is a sorcery card that costs one red mana and X (one or more) other color mana to cast. This card has the special ability of doing X damage to any one target creature. The damage X is set equal to the toughness rating on the target card. This is a very nice capability, because you don't have to worry about the toughness rating of the target card since X will always match it. If the target creature dies in the current turn, it is removed from the game entirely and sent to the graveyard.

Red also has easy artifact destruction abilities with the *Shatter* and *Shatterstorm* cards. And red is strong in removing land cards. The major weakness of red is its lack of ability to remove enchantments. Red does not have destructive capabilities and possesses very limited ability to regain lost life points. Some powerful red cards are *Shivan Dragon* and *Rock Hydra*.

Green: Life

The color green provides the greatest level of creature healing. Green cards are strong in creating illusions that they are harmless only to foil their opponents by powerful spells and special effects.

The first card, *Scryb Sprites*, is a Summon Faeries card that costs only one green mana to cast. It has a power/toughness rating of 1/1. When successfully cast, it is automatically given the special ability of "flying." This means that it can only be destroyed by another attacking creature that also has flying ability.

The second card, *Wild Growth*, is an Enchant Land card that costs one green mana to cast. Once successfully in play, it provides an additional point of mana whenever mana is drawn from a target land.

Green has the illusion of being peaceful and serene, only to surprise your opponent with a devastating arsenal of special effects. Green has the advantage in that it can generate creatures very quickly. Green also has an impressive array of enchantments. Green, however, lacks in the ability to deal damage directly to an opponent or a creature. It also lacks large flying creature cards. Some powerful green cards are *Living Artifact*, *Regeneration*, *Venom*, and *Scavenger Folk*.

Color:	*Green*
Name:	*Scryb Sprites*
Type:	*Summon Faeries*
Casting Cost:	*G*
Power/ Toughness:	*1/1*

Text

Flying (this card gains the special ability of flying).

Figure 4-9: *Scryb Sprites*, Summon Faeries

Color:	*Green*
Name:	*Wild Growth*
Type:	*Enchant Land*
Casting Cost:	*G*
Power/ Toughness:	*---*

Text

Gain one extra green mana when mana is drawn (tapped) from a target card.

Figure 4-10: *Wild Growth*, Enchant Land

Combining Colors

In constructing your playing deck, keep in mind that a deck that only has one color is seldom a very effective deck. This is because all colors are weak in least one area, and if you happen to play an opponent who has a color that is an enemy to yours and/or multiple colors, you will probably not fare too well. But, as with many other philosophies in Magic, this is not an absolute rule. If you put enough time and thought into constructing a deck with a single color, there is no reason why it could not be effective for you. On the other hand, when you construct your deck with different colors, you are really subtracting those weaknesses and summing their strengths. Much depends upon what your opponent has put together as to whether you will be effective in play.

Section 5

The Game Phases

The Various Magic Game Phases

A game of Magic is played by executing a series of sequential game phases. There are seven major phases. One of these, the Main phase, has three phases within it. All of the various game phases have been carefully constructed so the game can be played in an orderly equitable fashion for all players at all levels. Figure 5-1 shows the complete flow of a game of Magic.

Constructing Your First Game Deck

Your first step before you play a game is to have a deck of cards to play with. Constructing winning decks in Magic is a real art. When you first begin playing, don't worry about how effective your first few decks will be since you must play many games in order to be able to build the most effective decks. We suggest that you construct your first deck with cards of only two colors and add other color combinations as you become more experienced. Start with the colors red and black and build your deck so that it contains roughly one-third mana cards, one-third creature cards, and one-third interrupts, enchantments, sorceries, artifacts, and instants. This will allow you to get started playing.

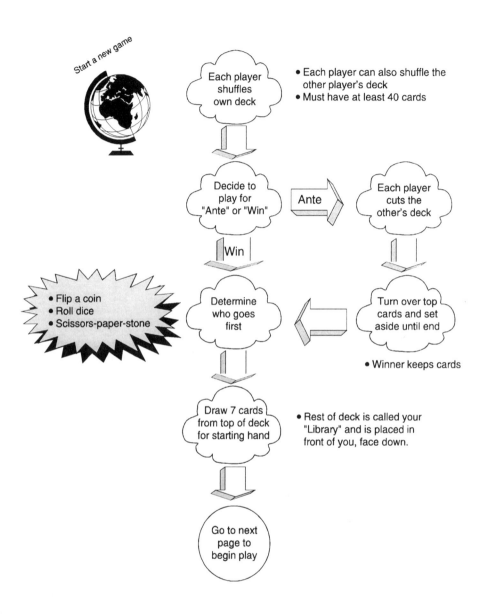

Start a new game

Each player shuffles own deck

• Each player can also shuffle the other player's deck
• Must have at least 40 cards

Decide to play for "Ante" or "Win"

Ante

Each player cuts the other's deck

Win

• Flip a coin
• Roll dice
• Scissors-paper-stone

Determine who goes first

Turn over top cards and set aside until end

• Winner keeps cards

Draw 7 cards from top of deck for starting hand

• Rest of deck is called your "Library" and is placed in front of you, face down.

Go to next page to begin play

Figure 5-1: Magic Game Flow (part 1)

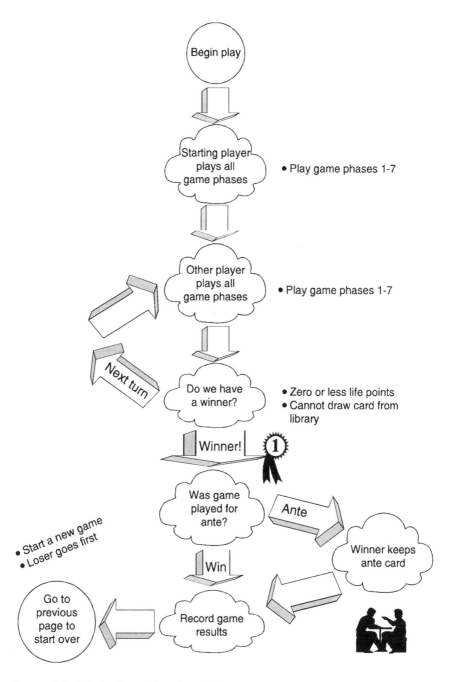

Figure 5-1: Magic Game Flow (part 2)

You will most likely need to purchase a few cards in order to form the starting deck recommended above. If you recall, starter decks contain forty cards and booster packs contain eight to fifteen cards. You probably need to purchase around 160 cards in order to have enough unique cards to build an effective starter deck. Of course, the more cards you buy, the greater your chances will be of obtaining additional unique cards.

How a Game of Magic Is Won

As mortals tell the story, Dominia is an immense, expansive place consisting of many lands, and the object of each player is to drive his or her opponent from the lands of Dominia. This is accomplished by playing a duel or Magic contest in which the winner can defeat his or her opponent in one of two ways:

1. Reducing opponent's starting twenty life points to zero or less.
2. Taking away the opponent's ability to draw a card from the deck (library).

This is not a place for those mere mortals who do not enjoy the rewards of a competitive duel! It is a place for combat, battle, confrontation, and crafty maneuvering. This is where you duel against your opponent. Only the strong or cunning person has the best chance of survival!

Pre-game Preparations

If you have a brief knowledge of Magic, you can turn to Section 6 which shows how to play a game. A Magic contest is started by first agreeing upon the rules and any special considerations such as who goes first, the sideboard, etc. Once these matters have been mutually agreed upon, both players shuffle their individual decks and then let the other shuffle their deck and cut it with a single card. Both decks are then placed face down in the respective library areas of each player's territory. If you are playing a game for *ante*, each player turns over the top card and sets it aside until the end of the duel. The winner gets to keep both cards. We recommend that you do not play for ante until you become more experienced.

Determine Who Goes First

Both players must now draw *seven* cards from their respective libraries. This forms your initial playing hand. If by chance, a player does not have any land or creature cards, then he or she can elect to reshuffle the deck. In this case, the player choosing to reshuffle the deck must also offer the option to his opponent.

The next step is to determine who goes first, a ritual common to nearly all games. If you are playing your opponent for the very first time, then this can be done by rolling dice, flipping a coin, or by any other method mutually agreed upon. If you have played a previous game with your opponent, then the person who lost the last game goes first.

Begin the Duel (Play a Game)

In playing a game of Magic, there are seven game phases that each player must complete during each turn in the course of the contest. Turns alternate until a winner is declared. Section 6 describes how a sample game of Magic is actually played.

A NOTE ABOUT RULE CHANGES

Although we have not specifically talked about rules, there are a number of rules that comprise Magic. As the game progresses over time and the number of cards increases, players and tournaments will likely cause some changes to the current rules. This is especially true in tournament play. Unlike the game of chess, which has survived generations with very few rule changes, Magic is approaching a half decade old and seasoned players have seen numerous changes to the rules.

The Seven Game Phases of Magic

Now that we have learned game terminology, the playing field, and some procedures for starting a game, we need to discuss the seven game phases and how they are executed. You can refer to Appendix A for a reference to these phases. Also, the card casting table below is helpful until you learn all game phases.

Card Type	When to Cast	Must Tap
Artifact	Main	Yes
Artifact-Creature	Main	Yes
Enchant	Main	Yes
Enchantment	Main	No
Instant[1]	Anytime	No
Interrupt[1]	Anytime	No
Land	Main	No
Sorcery[1]	Main	No
Summon (creature)	Main	Yes

[1] — Sent to the graveyard after being played.

The Untap Phase

Since you haven't played any cards in your first turn, this phase can be skipped. In your second and subsequent turns, you must untap any cards that have been tapped during your previous turn (unless they are blocked for some reason). Remember, untapping is the process of turning a card upright from its tapped or slanted position (Figure 2-2). This has the effect of informing your opponent that these cards have not yet been played. There are some cards which prevent you from tapping them but we will worry about this later. You might also note that no other cards can be played in this phase.

The Upkeep Phase

This phase is a little more involved because it depends upon what cards have been played during your previous turn. You might think of this phase as what it takes to keep certain cards that you wish to remain in play for your current turn. This is often called the "accounting" phase.

Some cards, after they have been successfully played, require that an upkeep cost be paid for the card to remain in play. For example, *Conversion* is an enchantment card that "forces all mountains to become plains! and costs two white mana (WW) during the upkeep phase in order to stay in play. If this upkeep is not covered, then it is removed from play and sent to the graveyard. In general, you can recognize a card that requires upkeep by the first item in the text portion of the card preceding a colon ":". If this item is a mana symbol or a circled number, then this is the amount of upkeep that must be paid to keep the card in play. Let's look at some examples. The card *Throne of Bone* is an artifact that has the number 1 circled in the text part of the card. This specifies an upkeep cost of one mana of any color. The card *Pestilence* is an enchantment which has one black mana symbol in the text. Therefore, its upkeep is one black mana to remain in play.

During this phase, there are other actions that can take place. One of these is that fast effects can be played by you during your opponent's turn. Remember, fast effects are card types such as instants, interrupts, and special abilities of permanents.

The Draw Phase

This phase is probably the simplest of all. In this phase, you must draw one card from the top of your library. You can then proceed to put it into your hand or in play. If you are unable to draw from your library, your opponent has defeated you! This is probably the most undesirable way to lose a game since you don't have too much control over cards in your library and you cannot really say that you were defeated with a great amount of skill. Remember, the other way your opponent can defeat you is to reduce your life points to zero or less. Fast effects can also be played during this phase.

The Main Phase

This phase is the most complicated phase of the game. First of all, it contains three phases within itself, and one of those phases, the Attack phase, contains a series of additional phases. The three main phases can be played in any order, and any individual phases can be skipped.

The three phases are:
1. Cast any type of spell such as artifacts, summons, enchantments, and sorceries.
2. Play only one land card.
3. Make one attack (cast a spell) against your opponent with one or more creature cards. Only fast effects can be played during the attack. The preferred sequence of events for an attack are:
   A. Announce that you are attacking. This allows either player to use any pre-attack fast effects.
   B. Declare and tap any attacking creatures.
   C. Either player plays fast effects.
   D. Declare blocking.
   E. Either player plays fast effects.
   F. Assign any damage.
   G. Either player uses regeneration, damage prevention, damage redirection, and life-giving fast effects. You can only use fast effects or interrupts.
   H. Send any creatures with lethal damage to the graveyard.
   I. Any effects that were caused by deaths such as Creature Bond damage, Vampires gaining counters, etc., take place. Fast effects not triggered by deaths cannot be played.

Phases B, D, F, and H occur immediately and you cannot use any fast effects. Steps F and I occur twice if they include any creatures with first strike capability.

The Discard Phase

Now that the major phases of your turn have been completed, it is time to reduce the total number of cards in your playing hand down to seven or less. Any discarded cards are sent directly to the graveyard. You can play fast effects during this phase if you have them. This is all there is to it for the Discard phase.

The End Phase

Sometimes called the "Inform Opponent" phase, this is simply a formality that lets your opponent know that you have finished with your turn. This should be done verbally. You can play fast effects if so desired.

The Heal Creatures Phase

This is the final phase of your turn. This means that any damage inflicted to creatures during the previous phases is removed (erased) and any fast effects expire. Until your next turn, this is the last chance you or your opponent has to play any fast effects. It is now your opponent's turn.

Section 6

Playing Magic

Introduction

This section demonstrates how to play a game of Magic. Since Magic has so many different playing situations, it would be impossible to describe all of them in this book. And it would be extremely difficult to show all the plays involved in a typical game. Therefore a typical game is illustrated, starting with the first move and progressing through a few basic turns. The section ends with an illustration of a variety of different playing combinations.

Playing a Few Rounds of Magic

The sample game presented here uses some of the more basic card types. A few simple examples allow you to master the basics of Magic play without worrying about numerous playing techniques and combinations.

After you have completed the preliminaries of a game, which include shuffling cards, cutting each other's deck, determining who goes first, and drawing seven cards from your library to form your starting playing hand, the very first move for each player is to play a card. Let's assume Player 1 won the right to go first. Remember, *we do not recommend that you play for ante until you feel you can play the game with a good level of confidence.*

Section 6

From this point on, we will describe a few moves of a sample game by using the following terms to denote each player's action:

Player: The player whose turn it is.
Move: One move in a player's turn.

Note that when the players switch from "player 1" to "player 2" or vice versa, this indicates the completion of a player's *turn* or seven game phases. By using this method to describe individual moves, it should easy to follow the game. So, let's begin playing Magic!

Here are both players' initial playing hands (player 1 chooses to play only two colors, blue and white, and player 2 red and black):

Player 1, Lacey _____

Plains	*Island*	*Island*	*Sea Serpent*
Type: Land	Type: Land	Type: Land	Type: Summon Serpent
			Color: Blue
			Cost: 5U (5 other, 1 blue)
			Power/Toughness: 5/5

Flight	*Disenchant*	*Healing Salve*
Type: Enchant	Type: Instant	Type: Instant
Creature	Color: White	Color: White
Color: Blue	Cost: 1W (1 other,	Cost: W (1 white)
Cost: U (1 blue)	1 white)	

Player 2, Jason _____

Mountain	*Mountain*	*Swamp*	*Summon Goblins*
Type: Land	Type: Land	Type: Land	Type: Summon Goblins
			Color: Red
			Cost: R (1 red)
			P/T: 1/1

Necrite	*Unholy Strength*	*Lightning Bolt*
Type: Summon	Type: Enchant Creature	Type: Instant
Thrull	Color: Black	Color: Red
Color: Black	Cost: B (1 black)	Cost: R (1 red)
Cost: 1BB (1 other, 2 black)		
P/T: 2/2		

54

Player 1: Move 1

In the very first turn of a duel, there are no cards in play and, therefore, the first two game phases, Untap and Upkeep, cannot be played but are not skipped. So Lacey's first move is to proceed to the Draw phase and draw one card from her library and put it into her hand. She now has eight cards.

Player 1: Move 2

Lacey's next move is to execute the Main phase. She must play a card that puts some mana into her mana pool. Cards that put mana into the mana pool are called "mana producing" cards. To do this, she plays an *Island*, which is a land card that puts one point of blue mana into her mana pool. She is now down to seven cards in her hand. She can now play a creature card that requires one point of blue mana if she has it in her hand. Unfortunately, she does not have a creature card that requires only one blue mana to cast. The *Sea Serpent* cannot be cast because it requires one blue mana and five mana of another color. Remember, you must play a creature card first before you can attack your opponent. And you must have creature cards in play in order to attack and cast spells on your opponent.

Player 1: Move 3

The Discard phase is next. Lacey must now check the total number cards she has in her hand, and if they exceed seven, discard any cards over seven. In this case, she has exactly seven cards so she does not discard any. Remember, even though she is unable to discard, she still must play the phase.

Since Lacey is now done with her turn, she must announce this fact to her opponent by saying "I'm finished" or something similar (Inform phase). The last phase, Heal Creatures, is also not executed at this point since she has not played any cards that could have inflicted damage on anyone. So, it is now her opponent's turn. During her turn, Lacey has performed a total of three separate actions.

Player 2: Move 1

Jason is also unable to execute the Untap and Upkeep phases. He then draws a card from the library since it is also his first turn. He draws the *Dwarven Soldier*, which is a Summon Dwarf card. This card only requires two mana to cast, one red and one of another color. He now has eight cards in his hand.

Player 2: Move 2

Like Jason's opponent, Lacey, his next move is to execute the Main phase. Jason decides to play a *Mountain* land card, which adds one point of red mana to his mana pool. He has a total of one mana in his mana pool. He is now down to seven cards in his hand.

Player 2: Move 3

Jason then notices that the *Mons's Goblin Raiders* creature card requires only one point of red mana, so he casts it on one of the two *Mountain* cards in play. The *Mountain* card is then *tapped* to show that the mana has been drawn (released) from it. The action of tapping also indicates that the card has been played during this turn. This is all that Jason can do at this point. Remember, the first time you cast a creature card, you cannot attack with it. Jason skips the remaining phases and announces that he is done.

Player 1: Move 1

Lacey cannot execute the Untap (because she has no cards that are tapped) and the Upkeep phase. She then draws a card from the library and gets the *Voldalian Soldiers*, which is a Summon Merfolk card. This is good news for Lacey because this card only requires one point of blue mana and one of another color to cast. She will be able to cast this color next turn.

Player 1: Move 2

Lacey decides to play a *Plains* card to add one point of white mana to her mana pool. She now has a total of two mana in her pool, one white and one blue. She is still unable to cast any creatures so she declares that she is done. The Heal Creatures phase cannot be executed again because no other cards have been played.

Player 2: Move 1

Jason skips the first two phases and draws another card from his library. He draws the *Wall of Stone*, which is a Summon Wall card. He will save this card for later. He then decides to play another Mountain land card which now gives him two red mana.

Player 2: Move 2

He now casts the *Dwarven Soldier* card on one of the *Mountain* cards and taps the *Mountain* card. Jason is now frustrated; Lacey does not have any creature cards in play so he is unable to launch an attack with his *Mons's Goblin Raiders* card. He will just have to be patient! Jason announces that he is done.

Game Summary

The above game plays demonstrate how to start a game of Magic and a couple of typical moves. Lacey was only able to play two land cards. Jason was a little more fortunate, as he was able to play two lands and two creatures. But neither player was able to initiate an attack or an action that would reduce the other's life points. A few more plays, though, could radically change this situation.

The remainder of this section will show a series of different plays using various card types and situations. The reader should pay close attention to what can and cannot be done in different playing situations.

Game Playing Scenarios

The previous section demonstrates how to start playing a typical game of Magic and how a few hands would be played. We will finish this section by selecting a series of play situations called "play scenarios" that illustrate how each of the different types of Magic cards are played. We will also show many of the various play combinations that can arise in Magic.

Each play scenario will have three parts:
1. Cards in play: Example of possible cards in your and/or your opponent's playing territory before you make your next move.
2. Your move: The card(s) you will play as described in the "play narrative."
3. Play narrative: Description of how each card is played and any supporting information that helps illustrate how the game, in general, is played. The part entitled "Dueler's Tidbits" gives general playing information about rules and maneuvering.

The narrative for each play scenario exhibits how each type of card is played along with other cards and play combinations to further illustrate various play situations.

Since there are so many possible game playing situations in Magic, we will only present a handful of plays that illustrate the various aspects of the game. You should review each play scenario carefully to get the most benefit.

Play Scenario #1: Play a land card for mana.

Your cards in play:
    Plains
    Type: Land

Your move:
    Plains
    Type: Land

Play Narrative

1. You have one land card in play and have one white mana. Your opponent might also have some land cards and other cards in play.
2. In the Main phase of your turn, you choose to play a land (*Plains*) card that can add one point of white mana to your mana pool, thereby giving you a total of two mana. The act of playing this card is said to "generate one point of white mana."
3. Since you do not have any creatures in play, you announce that your turn is over. Remember, you must have one or more creature cards in play in order to attack or cast a spell against your opponent.

Dueler's Tidbits

A. Mana is said to always be "colorless." This is because mana can be changed to different colors with the effects of other cards. When a mana-producing card is first played, it always generates the type of mana (colored or colorless) that is specified on the card. It is only afterward that it becomes colorless.
B. In turns to follow, you should attempt to play a creature card on one of your lands so that you are in the position to initiate an attack on your opponent. The sooner you do this, the better, so you can begin reducing your opponent's life points and be on your way toward winning the duel. After all, this is most likely what your opponent is planning to do to you!
C. When you play a land card such as the Plains card above, you don't tap it at this time because you have not used its abilities, i.e., you haven't played a creature card on it. The next game scenario illustrates tapping and how to bring a creature card into play.
D. Don't be fooled into thinking that once you have played a land card that there is no danger that could follow! There is always danger lurking somewhere in Magic! Your opponent could be lurking behind the bushes and play an instant or interrupt card that could destroy your land(s) and inflict numerous other types of damage.

Play Scenario #2: Play a creature card for the first time.

Your cards in play:

Forest	*Forest*	*Mountain*	*Mountain*
Type: Land	Type: Land	Type: Land	Type: Land

Island
Type: Land

Argothian Treefolk
Type: Summon Treefolk
Color: Green
Cost: 3GG (3 other, 2 green)
P/T: 3/5

Your move:
Elven Riders
Type: Summon Riders
Color: Green
Cost: 3GG (3 other, 2 green)
P/T: 3/3

Play Narrative

1. You have five land cards of three different color mana in play. Your opponent might also have some land cards and other cards in play.
2. You cast (play) *Elven Riders* on two green (GG) and three other color mana cards. To do this, you must use the two *Forest* cards and then choose any other three land cards, say two *Mountains* and one *Island*. You *draw* the mana out of the land cards in order to play the one creature card.
3. You might also be aware that this is a fairly expensive card to cast since it requires so much mana.

Dueler's Tidbits

A. The *Elven Riders* is a green summon card from the Legends card set. It has the special ability (described in the text portion of the card) that **it can only be blocked by creatures that are walls or flying**. This means that if you decide to launch an attack against your opponent with this card, your opponent cannot block it by any creatures except ones that are walls or flying. Walls and flying are two special abilities that some cards, such as the *Wall*

---

of *Wood* and *Dancing Scimitar*, have that can be used to defend against attacks.

B. This card also has a power (attack) ability of 3 and a toughness (defense) of 3, which is fair but not great. If your opponent attacks you with a creature having a power of 3 or above, the *Elven Riders* dies. The power rating for most cards ranges from 0 to 10. There is also no upkeep for this card to stay in play, another advantage.

Play Scenario #3: Play more than one creature card for the first time.

Your cards in play:

Plains	*Plains*	*Island*
Type: Land	Type: Land	Type: Land

Mountain	*Island*
Type: Land	Type: Land

Your move:

Combat Medic	*Apprentice Wizard*	*Island*
Type: Summon Soldier	Type: Summon Wizard	Type: Land
Color: White	Color: Blue	
Cost: 2W	Cost: 1UU (1 other, 2 blue)	
(2 other, 1 white)	P/T: 0/1	
P/T: 0/2		

Play Narrative

1. You have five mana in your pool: two white, two blue, and one red. Your opponent might also have some land cards and other cards in play.

2. You want to play both the *Combat Medic* and *Apprentice Wizard* creature cards. But this requires six mana and you are shy one land card. So your first move is to play another land card, say an *Island*. You now have a total of six land cards, enough to cast your two creature cards.

3. You now cast the *Combat Medic* on one white and two other lands. This card has the special ability of **preventing one point of damage to any player or creature** but has an upkeep of one white and one other mana.

4. You cast the *Apprentice Wizard* on two blue lands and one other. The *Combat Medic* card has the special ability to **prevent one damage to any player or creature**, but it requires an upkeep of one white mana (1W) in order to stay in play.

5. You tap all six cards to indicate they have been played.

Dueler's Tidbits

A. The *Apprentice Wizard* card is a good card to play as it adds three colorless mana to your mana pool and only requires one point of blue mana to get three colorless. But one of its disadvantages is that it must be tapped when played and has a very shabby attack and defense capability of 0/1. The primary advantage of playing this card is to add to your mana pool.

Play Scenario #4: Play an enchant creature card.

Your cards in play:

Goblin King	*Plains*	*Mountain*	*Mountain*
Type: Summon	Type: Land	Type: Land	Type: Land
Goblin King			
Color: Red		*Plains*	
Cost: 1RR (1 other, 2 red)		Type: Land	
P/T: 2/2			

Your move:

> *Eternal Warrior*
> Type: Enchant Creature
> Color: Red
> Cost: R

Play Narrative

1. You have two white land cards, two red land cards, and the *Goblin King* creature card in play.
2. Your next move is to play the *Eternal Warrior* on the *Goblin King*.
3. Tap both cards. This card has the ability of **not having to be tapped when it attacks**. This is a fairly powerful capability that allows this creature to attack and act as if it had never been played. This process is called "pumping" a card.

Dueler's Tidbits

A. When you play an enchant creature card, you can think of it as having "enchanted" the inherent abilities of the card that it is played on, thereby giving it a more powerful playing ability or reducing its playability.
B. In general, enchantment cards fall into two basic categories: "enchant *something*" and "enchantment." When you cast a card that says enchant *something*, it must be played on a card of the appropriate type as described by *something*, and the target card can be one of yours or your opponent's. Once the card is cast, it stays in play until the card it was cast on no longer exists, in which case the enchant card is discarded. The other type of enchantment, called enchantment, also stays in play. Both types of enchantments can only be played in the Main phase and are never tapped.
C. A special case of an enchantment is the *Enchant Enchantment* spell, which can be cast on any other enchantment or enchant *something* card. For example, if I play *Power Leak* on my opponent's *Unholy Strength*, then an upkeep of 2 will be required to keep *Unholy Strength* in play; otherwise my opponent suffers one point of damage for each point of unpaid mana.

Play Scenario #5: Play an enchant land card.

Your cards in play:

Fallen Angel	*Swamp*	*Swamp*	*Forest*
Type: Summon Angel	Type: Land	Type: Land	Type: Land
Color: Black			
Cost: 3BB (3 other, 2 black)			
P/T: 3/3			

Forest	*Forest*	*Plains*
Type: Land	Type: Land	Type: Land

Your move:

Evil Presence
Type: Enchant Land
Color: Black
Cost: B

Play Narrative

1. You have six land cards (two black mana, three green mana, one white) and a *Fallen Angel* creature in play.
2. You play *Evil Presence* on a land card.
3. Tap *Evil Presence* and the corresponding land card.

Dueler's Tidbits

A. The enchant land card is similar in effect to the other enchant cards: it normally enhances the playability of designated cards in play.
B. This could be a very good move to make if your opponent is not playing the color black because it would prevent him from adding to the black mana in his mana pool and bringing black creatures into play. On the other hand, if your opponent is already playing black and you pick a land of a different color to turn into a swamp, it could have the detrimental effect of increasing the black mana pool just enough, thereby allowing your opponent to play a potentially dangerous creature card.
C. You must study each play situation very carefully and weigh all the possibilities before you make your move. Remember that elusive and random element of "chance" can easily make or spoil your day!

Play Scenario #6: Play an enchantment card.

Your cards in play:

Drudge Skeletons	Island	Swamp	Plains
Type: Summon Skeletons	Type: Land	Type: Land	Type: Land
Color: Black		Island	Plains
Cost: 1B (1 other, 1 black)		Type: Land	Type: Land
P/T: 1/1			

Your move:

Lifeblood
Type: Enchantment
Color: White
Cost: 2WW (2 other, 2 white)

Play Narrative

1. In your Main phase you play the *Lifeblood*, which costs two white and two other mana, and tap both cards. *Lifeblood* has the special ability that **each time one of your opponent's mountains is tapped, you gain one additional life point**.

Dueler's Tidbits

A. Remember, enchantments cannot be tapped. The "enchantment" card is played in the caster's territory, where the "enchant *creature*" card must be played on the appropriate card type (normally a creature card).

B. If the card on which an enchant or enchantment is played ceases to exist or is no longer a valid target, then the enchantment is discarded.

Play Scenario #7: Play a sorcery card.

Your cards in play:

Forest	*Island*	*Island*	*Island*
Type: Land	Type: Land	Type: Land	Type: Land

Your move:

Amnesia	*Forest*
Type: Sorcery	Type: Land
Color: Blue	
Cost: 3UU (3 other, 2 blue)	

Play Narrative

1. You have four land cards in play, one green and three blue. You play another *Forest* card and then follow with the *Amnesia* sorcery card, which costs two blue and three other mana.
2. Tap the five land cards. The *Amnesia* card allows you to **look at your opponent's hand and force him or her to discard all non-land cards.**

Dueler's Tidbits

A. This is an extremely effective card, as it removes any potentially damaging cards from your opponent's hand.
B. Another good sorcery card to play is the *Jovial Evil*, which **inflicts two points of damage on your opponent for each white creature card that he or she currently controls.**
C. Another example of a good sorcery card is the *Martyr's Cry*, which costs only two white mana to cast but has the horrifying effect of **removing all white creatures from both players' territory.** After this unfortunate event takes place, both players must then draw one card for each white creature that they control and that was removed.
D. A final example is the *Raise Dead* card that allows you to **bring one creature of your choice from your graveyard into your hand.**
E. Sorcery cards in general can be rather nasty and intimidating and quite often affect the outcome of the game.

Play Scenario #8: Play an interrupt card.

Your cards in play:

Plains	*Plains*	*Mountain*
Type: Land	Type: Land	Type: Land

Your move:

Desert Nomads	*Dark Ritual*	*Swamp*
Type: Summon Nomads	Type: Interrupt	Type: Land
Color: Red	Color: Black	
Cost: 2R (2 other, 2 red)	Cost: B	
P/T: 2/2		

Play Narrative

1. You have three mana of two colors and the *Desert Nomads* creature card. You then play another *Swamp* card to increase your mana pool.
2. You then decide to initiate an attack. You announce that you are attacking with the *Desert Nomads* and tap it. If your opponent cannot block it with a card defense of two or greater, then he or she suffers two points of damage.
3. If your opponent decides to block *Desert Nomads* with a card that has a defense of two, then he or she suffers no damage.
4. You then respond by playing the *Dark Ritual* interrupt, which adds back three black mana to your mana pool. You must then remove this card from the game.

Dueler's Tidbits

A. An interrupt can be played during your turn or your opponent's turn and is discarded after being played. The effect that it might have on another spell is permanent. But it should be noted that interrupts can no longer be played once a player has taken any other game action that is not casting an interrupt.

Play Scenario #9: Play an instant card.

Your cards in play:

Island	*Plains*	*Plains*
Type: Land	Type: Land	Type: Land

Devouring Deep
Type: Islandwalk
Color: Blue
Cost: 2U (2 other, 1 blue)
P/T: 1/2

Enchanted Being
Type: Summon Being
Color: White
Cost: 1WW
P/T: 2/2

Your move:
Festival
Type: Instant
Color: White
Cost: W

Play Narrative

1. You play the *Festival* instant immediately, which **prevents your opponent from launching an attack when it is his or her turn.**
2. You must play this card during your opponent's **Upkeep phase.**
3. Instants cannot cancel or interrupt other instants.

Dueler's Tidbits

A. Another effective instant is the *Mana Short* which forces your opponent to **tap all lands in play and then clears his or her mana pool.**
B. The *Reverse Damage* card could be a lifesaver if it is played at the right moment. This card **takes any damage that you have taken from any single card and adds it to your total life points.**

Play Scenario #10: Play an artifact card.

Your cards in play:

Lord of the Pit	*Island*	*Island*
Type: Summon Demon	Type: Land	Type: Land
Color: Black		
Cost: 4BBB (4 other, 3 black)		
P/T: 7/7		

Your move:

Life Chisel
Type: Artifact
Color: ---
Cost: 4

Play Narrative

1. You have two *Island* cards and the *Lord of the Pit* in play.
2. You decide to play the *Life Chisel* artifact on the *Lord of the Pit*. Before *Lord of the Pit* is sacrificed, the **caster gains seven life points** (its toughness rating).

Dueler's Tidbits

A. Although this boosts your life points by seven, it requires the sacrifice of a card that has a very high attack and defense rating. If you have other creature cards in play when this type of play combination occurs, you might want to use a card with a lower toughness rating so you don't lose your *Lord of the Pit* card.

Play Scenario #11: Play an artifact creature card.

Your cards in play:

Desert Nomads	***Plains***	***Forest***
Type: Summon Nomads	Type: Land	Type: Land
Color: Red		
Cost: 2R (2 other, 2 red)		
P/T: 2/2		

Your move:

Clay Statue
Type: Artifact Creature
Color: ---
Cost: 4
P/T: 3/1

Play Narrative

1. Your opponent kills your *Desert Nomads* with an instant and sends it to the graveyard.
2. If you have two colorless mana, it can be regenerated and returned to play.

Dueler's Tidbits

1. The *Clay Statue* can also be sent to the graveyard if it receives lethal damage.
2. A card that is regenerated must always come back into play tapped.

Play Scenario #12: Attack with banding.

Your cards in play:

Benalish Hero	**Phantasmal Forces**	**Island**
Type: Summon Hero	Type: Summon Phantasm	Type: Land
Color: White	Color: Blue	
Cost: W (1 white)	Cost: 3U (3 other, 1 blue)	
P/T: 1/1	P/T: 4/1	

Island	**Plains**	**Plains**	**Plains**
Type: Land	Type: Land	Type: Land	Type: Land

Your move:

Benalish Hero	**Phantasmal Forces**
Type: Summon Hero	Type: Summon Phantasm
Color: White	Color: Blue
Cost: W	Cost: 3U
P/T: 1/1	P/T: 4/1

Play Narrative

1. You initiate an attack with *Benalish Hero* and *Phantasmal Forces* by banding them together. This can be done because one of the creatures has banding ability, namely *Benalish Hero*. *Phantasmal Forces* requires one blue mana of upkeep to stay in play or it is destroyed. You choose which defending target creature dies if your opponent decides to put up a defense.
2. Your opponent must decide how to defend against these cards.

Dueler's Tidbits

A. If you attack with two creatures that are banded together, such as above, then you choose which one of your opponent's defending creatures dies (if any). Remember, your opponent can choose to defend with one or two cards (or no cards).
B. If you attack and your opponent defends with two creatures that are banded, then your opponent chooses which creature dies (if any).

Section 7

Trading Cards

Introduction

Trading Magic cards can become an important part of your overall game strategy, or it can simply become something fun to do. Whatever your goal is, you should know the basic concepts of trading cards and the various tradeoffs that suit your objectives.

Types of Traders

All card traders fall into two basic categories: players and collectors.

A person who values cards that are good in *play* will most likely never sacrifice the ability to play a card for its rarity or some other aspect of the card such as the picture or card theme. You should be aware that this type of player is probably experienced and mainly concerned with building up his or her arsenal of cards. Therefore, you should know the value of your cards and which ones you do not want to trade. This type of trader will not care too much about the condition of the card unless it is one that is in a collection.

The person who *collects* Magic cards will place a great deal of importance on the value and condition of a card. The condition is rated from *very fine* to *mint*. You might be able to get a good deal from a person who collects cards, as he might be more likely to give you more value if he needs a card that you possess for his collection. This, of course, depends upon the individual. Some people are both players and collectors, and their trading objectives might be quite different. But be aware of the "sharks" who trade cards for both collection and making money. These traders will be more cunning, and you should trade cautiously with them!

Trading Skills

When trading cards, you should have a set of trading skills that will allow you to trade effectively. These are:

1. Have a plan or deck theme.
2. Know the monetary value of cards.
3. Have a published price list.
4. Know what the other person wants.

The first skill—have a plan—refers to knowing what you are trading for. You should know what cards that you would like to keep for your game or collection and which ones you would be willing to trade. The second skill—knowing what cards are worth—is probably the most important aspect of trading. Knowing the price of Magic cards is similar to knowing the prices of goods when you go shopping. No matter what your trading objectives are or how experienced a player you are, you should always have a good idea of the current value of cards. Although the value of a card is more useful in collecting cards than in playing them, it is important to know the values for overall trading ability. This brings us to the third skill—have a published price list. Until you know prices by heart, carry an up-to-date price list of cards with you when trading. This will allow you to trade in confidence. You should also be aware that the price of a card, and sometimes its rarity, depends upon the geographical area where you live. Due to availability, cards which are rare or expensive in one town may be just the opposite in another community.

Card Value

The value of a card is an important aspect to master as a trader. There are four different categories:

1. Rarity
2. Playability
3. Price
4. Personal value

These four factors determine the real and aesthetic value of a Magic card. The *rarity* is determined based on the total number of cards that were printed by the manufacturer and is rated from U1(R) to C4(C), where R is rare and C is common. Cards are also rated by local groups, clubs, and organizations. A rare card is very valuable since it could be worth several uncommons or numerous commons, depending upon the trading situation. Rare cards are least known, and you should not make the mistake of equating rarity with power of play. For example, if we compare the *Benalish Hero*, a white common card, to the *Timber Wolves*, a green rare card, they appear to be identical except for the color. What separates them is the fact that the green *Timber Wolves* card has banding special ability, which is uncommon for the color green, and was the only card of its type in the Revised Edition. This is one of the aspects that makes it rare.

The *playability* of a card is simply a rating of how good it is in play. In general, the better the playability of a card, the more trade value it will have. The *price* of a card is determined by the Magic card playing population. There are two types of pricing systems: national and local. The local system is most commonly used by dealers and traders.

Lastly, the *personal value* of a card refers to the personal reasons why a player or collector wishes to have a card. Maybe the person likes to collect cards with dragons or monsters on them, or he is building a certain type of card collection. These are all reasons for attaching a personal value to a card.

Concluding Remarks

Trading Magic cards is one of the most important aspects of the game and increases its overall value and popularity. When you decide to trade a card, all you need to do is use your common sense and consider the suggestions above, and your trading experiences will most likely be pleasant ones. If you are not secure in your trading ability, bring an experienced friend with you.

Section 8

Playing in Tournaments

Introduction

This section describes what tournament play is all about and how to prepare yourself for Magic tournaments.

Playing in Magic tournaments can be good for your game. But you must be ready to play in a highly structured competitive environment where there are very specific rules and regulations that must be followed. When you are playing in tournaments, you tend to meet players that you have not played before, and the intensity of play is much greater. All in all, the thrill of your first tournament will be something that you will remember for a long time to come.

The Duelists' Convocation

Although in concept, a Magic tournament can be just a gathering of people at a local game store, official sanctioned tournaments are frequently scheduled around the world. The organization that governs all Magic: The Gathering™ tournaments and other official events is the Duelists' Convocation. This is a player's membership organization, run by Wizards of the Coast, which gives players an opportunity to participate in weekly league activities at their local game stores and offers a flock of other opportunities in card trading, dueling, and refining your deck-building skills. Stores that are active will offer a more complete range of activities such as guest appearances, lectures, special promotional items, etc. At sanctioned gaming tournaments, you can obtain up-to-date information on rules and new expansion card sets, and participate in other scheduled events. Most of this information can also be obtained on the Magic home page on the Internet.

Playing for National Ranking

One of the benefits of playing in tournaments is that you can compete for prizes and gain points that count toward your national ranking. If you play in enough tournaments, you can eventually gain ranking at the national level. A newsletter called *The Duelist's Companion* contains current information on convocation news and events in general.

Types of Tournaments

There are three types of Magic: The Gathering convocation tournaments that are officially sanctioned:

Tournament Type	Playing Characteristics	Card Sets Used
Type I	Referred to as a "constructed deck" tournament in which you may use any cards that official tournament rules allow.	Magic: The Gathering Arabian Nights Antiquities Legends The Dark Fallen Empires Ice Age
Type II	Same as Type I but places a greater restriction on card usage.	Magic: The Gathering The Dark[1] Fallen Empires[1] Ice Age[1]
Sealed Deck	Played with a limited card pool without trading.	Sealed decks

[1] - Always the latest two expansion card sets.

Table 8-1. Magic: The Gathering Tournament Types

The idea behind having different types of tournaments is to give the game a greater challenge and offer more variety in officially sanctioned activities. Although each type of tournament offers different deck construction rules, a standard set of floor rules applies to all tournaments.

Rules for Type I and Type II tournaments are same as the official tournament rules (see below). For Sealed Deck tournaments, some rules vary slightly:

1. Play with a minimum of forty cards with no imposed maximum.
2. Can change number of cards in playing deck and sideboard.
3. There are no restricted or banned cards.
4. Decks are constructed using one sealed deck (sixty cards) of the latest Magic: The Gathering edition and one of the following additions:
   A. Three sealed booster packs of the latest eight-card booster pack Limited Edition expansion set, a total of eighty-four cards.
   B. Two sealed booster packs of the latest fifteen-card booster pack Limited Edition expansion sets, a total of ninety cards.
   C. Two sealed booster packs of the latest Magic: The Gathering edition, a total of ninety cards.

You must choose which type of tournament you would like to participate in as a beginning player. As you become a more experienced player, you will probably want to try each type of tournament or organize your own.

Official Tournament Rules

The following are rules that are used in officially sanctioned Magic: The Gathering tournaments. You should be aware that these rules are not cast in concrete and can change at any time to support the latest expansion card sets.

The officially sanctioned tournament rules for play and deck construction are as follows:

1. Any *rule violation* may be interpreted by the judge as a *Declaration of Forfeiture*. This right is non-negotiable.
2. All *disagreements* are settled by the tournament judge.

3. A *duel* is one complete game of Magic in which there is a declared winner.

4. A *match* consists of the *best two out of three duels* for standard rounds, and the *best three out of five duels* for semifinal and final rounds.

5. A tournament *playing deck* consists of at least *sixty cards* which can include lands, creatures, spells, and artifacts.

6. A player must use the *same playing deck* for the entire tournament.

7. A *sideboard* of exactly *fifteen cards* is optional and must be declared and mutually agreed upon by both players before the start of a duel. Cards can only be exchanged between the playing deck and the sideboard on a *one-to-one* basis *between duels or matches*, and any number of cards, up to fifteen, can be exchanged at once. Each player must allow the other to count, face down, the number of cards in the sideboard.

8. No playing deck can contain more than *four of any individual card*, including the sideboard, with the exception of the five basic land types (Forest, Island, Mountain, Plains, Swamp).

9. The playing deck can contain only one card from the *Restricted List*. At the end of a duel, each player must show the remaining cards of his or her hand, graveyard, and all other piles of cards to verify that no Restricted List duplicate cards were played. The Restricted List is different for Type I and Type II tournaments and does not apply to Sealed Deck tournaments.

10. Playing a tournament for *ante* is optional and must be mutually agreed on by both players before the start of a duel.

11. A player may not play with any card from the *banned* list. The banned list is different for Type I and Type II tournaments and does not apply to Sealed Deck tournaments.

12. You cannot use any cards from any of the Collector's Editions (square corners and gold trim).

13. Cards in your playing hand must, at all times, be kept above the level of the playing surface (territory).

14. A player may not use outside assistance during a match. One warning will be given before the Judge considers a Declaration of Forfeiture.

15. *Proxy* cards are not allowed. A proxy card is a card that is used represent another card that a player wishes not to play. This is done by writing the name of the card that you want to play on the proxy card.

16. If a player draws either no land cards or all lands cards on the initial draw of seven cards, then a *mulligan* can be declared and the duel may be restarted. The player calling a mulligan must show his or her hand, cut and reshuffle the deck, and draw new cards. The opponent also has this option even if his hand does not qualify for a mulligan.

As a final note, you should be aware that the Director of the Duelists' Convocation reserves the right to change any of the official Duelists' Convocation rules, with or without notice, at any time that it becomes necessary to do so.

Section 9

Effective Card Combinations

Introduction

This section introduces the concept of developing effective "card combinations." Just like the process in constructing winning decks, card combinations can be a good technique to help you win games. Although this is considered to be an advanced part of Magic, we believe it deserves your attention.

What Is a Card Combination?

A card combination is defined to be two or more cards that are combined together to form a more effective play situation. Some combinations have only two cards and others have as many as four or five. In the list below, I have shown a number of card combinations that are my personal favorites. The list is alphabetized by the first card name. The reader is encouraged to look at each card within a given combination and determine how and why it could be used as an effective playing combination. Remember, you cannot rely on when any given card combination that you have shuffled into your library will be available to play. All you can do is hope that you will have a chance to play a combination before your opponent destroys any of your cards.

The card combinations shown below were taken from the Internet Magic home page (see Appendix F). This is a good source for obtaining current information on not only card combinations but a wealth of other Magic card topics. Each card combination is listed along with the originator's name. Where there is not a recognized originator, the phrase "public knowledge" is used. If you wish to communicate by e-mail to enter your own combinations, or if you have questions, send them to *umnarqu4@cc.umanitoba.ca.*

Selected Card Combinations

A

Abu Ja Far + Lure	*Eric Plante*
Aisling Leprechaun + Green Ward	*Jonathan Dean*
Alabaster Potion + Reset	*Kathleen Cully*
Aladdin + Dwarven Weaponsmith	*The Jester*
Aladdin + Orcish Mechanics	*Robert Barry*
Ali From Cairo + Jade Monolith	*Mark Rosewater*
Animate Artifact + Instill Energy + Time Vault	*public knowledge*
any creature + Holy Armor + Life Chisel	*Mitch Burton*
any Mox or Sol Ring (opponent's) + Artifact Possession	*The Mist*
Argivian Archaeologist + Chaos Orb	*Ichabod*
Argivian Archaeologist + Juggernaut or Black Lotus	*Alex*
Armageddon Clock + Dingus Egg + Mana Flare + Pyramids	*Peter Giffin*
Artifact Possession + Phyrexian Gremlins	*Michael Belrose*
Artifact Ward + Martyrs of Korlis	*Robert C. Rossel*
Ashnod's Altar + multiple Nether Shadows	*Saint Germain*
Aspect of Wolf + Gaea's Liege + Shanodin Dyrads	*Pete Giffin*
Atog + Onulet	*Paul Gyugyi*

B

Beasts of Bogardan + Deathlace	*Mitch Burton*
Berserk + Rukh's Egg + Giant Growth	*Rainer Dittman*
Bird of Paradise + Instill Energy	*Robert Barry*
Black Vise + Braingeyser	*Cindi Suriano & Jeff Naiman*

Blue Elemental Blast + Chaoslace   *Michael Belrose*

C

Candelabra of Twanos + Power Surge   *Alex*
Castle + The Hive   *Greg Porter*
Circle of Protection: Red + Orcish Artillery   *Jeff Naiman*
Colossus of Sardia + Instill Energy   *Mark Rosewater*
Copper Tablet + Living Artifact   *Peter Donald*
Creature Bond + Jump + Earthbind   *Jameel Alkhafiz*
Cyclone or Pestilence + Fungusaur   *Toby Elliott*

D

Deathlace + Beasts of Bogardan   *Mitch Burton*
Diamond Valley + Granite Gargoyle   *Marvin Goldberg*
Dingus Egg + Armageddon + Reverse Damage   *Robert Barry*
Disintegrate or Fireball + Channel   *public knowledge*
Drop of Honey + Khabal Ghoul   *Toby Elliott*
Dwarven Warriors + Firebreathing   *Jeff Naiman*

E

Earthquake (1 point) + Kormus Bell   *Mike Aparicio*
Eye for an Eye + Reverse Damage   *Pete Giffin*

F

Fastbond + Circle of Protection: Green   *Eric Plante*
Fireball or Disintegrate + Channel   *public knowledge*
Firebreathing + Uthden Troll + Lure   *Sven Helmer*
Fork + Demonic Tutor   *Bob Vines*

G

Gaea's Leige + Lifetap   *Paul Pantera*
Giant Growth + Rukh's Egg + Berserk   *Rainer Dittman*
Glasses of Urza + Wheel of Fortune or   *Daniel Hamel*
        Mind Twist
Grapeshot Catapult + Jump   *Peter Donald*
Green Ward + Aisling Leprechaun   *Jonathan Dean*

H

Hell's Caretaker + Hive	*Kathleen Cully*
Howling Mine + Phyrexian Gremlins	*Saint Germain*
Hurkyl's Recall + Timetwister	*Edward Chen*

I

Icy Manipulator + Psychic Venom	*Cindi Suriano*
Icy Manipulator or Twiddle + Psychic Venom	*Mark Rosewater*
Instill Energy (optional) + Wrath of God + Khabal Ghoul	*Kathleen Cully*
Instill Energy + Ley Druid	*The Mist*

J

Jade Monolith + Ali From Cairo	*Mark Rosewater*
Jandor's Saddlebags + Sorceress Queen + Prodigal Sorcerer	*Edward Chen*

K

Karma + Magical Hack	*Red Adept*
Khabal Ghoul + Oubliette + Nevinyrral's Disk	*Matthew M. Messana*
Kormus Bell or Living Lands + Keldon Warlord	*Mark Rosewater*

L

Ley Druid + Library of Alexandria	*Jonathan Dane Cooke*
Library of Leng + Arboria + Ivory Tower	*Mitch Burton*
Lifeforce + Sleight of Mind	*Aaron*
Lifetap + Magical Hack	*Matthew M. Messana*
Llanowar Elves + Metamorphosis	*Peter Donald*
Lure + Regeneration + Infernal Medusa	*Mitch Burton*
Lure + Thicket Basilisk	*public knowledge*

M

Magical Hack + Karma	*Red Adept*
Mana Flare + Gauntlet of Might + Roc Hydra + Power Surge	*Mike Daniel*
Mind Twist + The Rack	*Daniel Hamel*
Mishra's Factory + Ley Druid	*Robert Barry*

N

Natural Selection + Demonic Attorney	*Peter Giffin*
Nevinyrral's Disk + Regrowth + Reconstruction	*David Schwartz*
Northern Paladin + Sleight of Mind	*Peter White*

O

Old Man of the Sea + Sorceress Queen	*Peter Donald*
Ornithopter + Argivan Archaeologist + Yawgmoth Demon	*The Jester*
Ornithopter + Unholy Strength	*Rob Vines*

P

Paralyze (multiple) + any creature	*Michael Belrose*
Pestilence + Living Lands	*Eric Robert Jablow*
Petra Sphinx + Zira Arien	*Mitch Burton*
Power Leak + Relic Bind + Sol Ring	*(hartman@ulogic.com)*
Power Surge + Circle of Protection: Red	*Larry Estep*
Power Surge + Candelabra of Tawnos	
Pyramids + Balance	*The Jester*

Q

Quarum Trench Gnomes + Moat	*Larry W. Smith*

R

Regrowth + Nevinyrral's Disk + Reconstruction	*David Schwartz*
Rocket Launcher + Guardian Beast	*Mile Daniel*
Royal Assassin + Icy Manipulator	*Lizard*
Royal Assassin + Paralyze	*Matthew Ault*
Rukh Egg + Stone Giant + Orcish Oriflamme (optional)	*Brian J. Wilson*

S

Shanodin Dryads + Gaea's Liege + Aspect of Wolf	*Peter Giffin*
Siren's Call + Icy Manipulator	*Candi Suriano*
Sol Ring or any Mox (opponent's) + Artifact Possession	*The Mist*
Stasis + Black Vise	*Jeff Naiman*

Stone Giant + Uthden Troll or Clay Statue   *Christopher G. Wood*

T
Tawnos's Wand or Dwarven Warriors +   *Jonathan Butler*
Frozen Shade or Pit Scorpion
The Hive or Master of Wolves + Lord of the Pit   *Jean-Francois Moyen*
Touch of Darkness + Hellfire   *Kathleen Cully*
Tsunami or Volcanic Eruption or Flash Fires +   *Eric Robert Jablow*
          Dingus Egg

U
Unsummon + Spell Block + Animate Dead   *public knowledge*
Unsummon + Wheel of Fortune   *Eric Robert Jablow*

V
Vampire Beast + Al-abara'a Carpet   *Larry W. Smith*

W
Will-O-The-Wisp (multiples) + Castle   *Greg Porter*
Winter Orb + Phyrexian Gremlins   *Saint Germain*
Wolverine Pack + Lure + Regeneration   *Mitch Burton*
Wrath of God or Nevinyrral's Disk + Unsummon   *Jameel Alkhafiz*

X
Xira Arien + Sylvan Library   *Mitch Burton*

Y
Yawgmoth Demon + The Hive   *Pete Giffin*

Z
Zephyr Falcon + Angry Mob   *Larry W. Smith*

Glossary of Terms

activation cost — The cost to trigger an effect of an artifact, creature, or enchantment. This is usually the cost of mana and/or tapping but there are other possible costs. This cost is written on the card as "cost: effect."

Alpha Edition — The original set of Magic cards, of which thirty-five were discontinued when the Revised Edition was released.

AN — Abbreviation for the Arabian Nights card edition.

ante — A Magic game in which both players wager (ante) the top card of their decks and the winner gets to keep both cards.

artifact — A basic spell type that can only be cast during the Main phase and used in the turn in which it is played. If the artifact is tapped, it cannot be used again until it is untapped. Some artifacts have a cost to use. If the artifact does not have a tap symbol or cost to use, then it is continuous and its effects are present until untapped.

artifact creature — An artifact that is also a creature; it is effected by anything that is an artifact or creature.

artifact removal capacity — The ability of a deck to remove artifacts from play.

Antiquities — The second expansion set of Magic cards based on the War of the Artificers. The set consists of one hundred unique cards, and nineteen of them were recirculated into the Revised Edition. The symbol for this set of cards is the anvil.

Arabian Nights	The first expansion set of Magic cards based on stories from *The Arabian Nights*. This set consists of seventy-eight unique cards, and twenty of them were recirculated into the Revised Edition. The symbol for this set of cards is the scimitar. Since fourteen of these cards have two variants, the set can really be considered to contain ninety-two total cards.
AQ	Abbreviation for the Antiquities card edition.
Attack phase	Part of the Main phase in which creatures can attack the opposing sorcerer.
attacking creature	Any creature that is attacking an opponent's creature, tapped or not.
banding	The special ability that allows a creature to combine with other creatures to form a defense or attack. This ability can be divided into mutual assistance and damage sharing.
banned list	List of cards that have been banned from official convocation tournaments because they require ante for playing. They can be played in non-tournament games.
basic land	One of the basic land card types, such as Plains (white mana), Islands (blue mana), Mountains (red mana), Forests (green mana), and Swamps (black mana).
Beta Edition	The original set of Magic cards that were printed and released on October 4, 1993. This set contained corrections from the Alpha Edition.
black	One of the five colors of Magic that represents death. Black gets its power from Swamps and Bogs, and its traditional enemies are green and white magic.
bleeder deck	A deck constructed in such a manner that it prevents an opponent from playing cards at every opportunity and buries them as soon as they are obtained.
block	One of three groups of twenty cards that make up a sixty-card tournament deck. Each block represents one-third of a deck and contains five pockets.
blue	One of the five colors of Magic that represents the mind or mental magic. Blue gets its power from Islands, and its traditional enemies are red and green.

booster pack | A pack of Magic cards smaller than a starter deck that contains eight to fifteen cards. Starter decks normally contain forty cards.

buried | A term used to denote a card that is sent to the graveyard without the possibility of being regenerated.

burn deck | A deck designed to quickly remove all of an opponent's life with direct damage spells.

card | Any Magic card that does not include creatures that are represented by tokens rather than cards.

card drawing capacity | The ability of a deck to draw more cards than those drawn during the Draw phase.

Care Bear Magic | Situation in multi-player Magic where everyone refuses to attack one another.

characteristics (of a creature) | This refers to the individual characteristics of a card such as type, color, power, toughness, casting cost, and special abilities of a creature. If the creature has any enchantments, they do not count toward its characteristics.

Collector's Edition | A special set of Magic cards that was distributed as a complete set. There were only 10,000 printed and they have square corners. These cards cannot be played in donvocation tournaments.

color | The spell color of a card such as blue, black, green, red, and white. The borders of a card normally indicate the color of the spell. In most cases, the color of a spell is determined by the color of mana used to cast the spell. Some spells may change the color of another spell or card as indicated in the description portion.

colorless | Cards such as artifacts and lands that are colorless if not one of the five colors. Artifacts produce colorless mana. If a spell does not require a color, then it is colorless and is represented by gray circle with a number inside. This type of card can use any color of mana.

continuous | Refers to effects that apply all the time; identified by the absence of a cost. In order to stop this type of card, you must get rid of it.

controller | The player who is controlling a card in play, usually the player who cast the spell.

convocation	The official organization for players as developed by Wizards of the Coast. This is also referred to as the Duelists' Convocation.
cost (of a spell)	The amount of mana required to cast a spell, displayed in the upper right corner of a card.
counter	Either some sort of marker to keep track of charges or special effects of a spell, or a means to cancel a spell before it can take effect. If a spell is countered, then all mana that was used to cast the spell is wasted and the card is sent to the graveyard. An Interrupt is the only card that can counter a spell.
counter ability	The "counter ability" of a deck is the most effective measure to stop an opposing player from utilizing his or her deck to the fullest capacity. All counters are played as interrupts, and one must usually stop an action while it is being cast, an ineffective counter to special land cards. This also will tie up mana because it is a reaction to the opposing player's spell.
counter deck	A deck that is designed mainly around counter cards and their ability to halt your opponent's plans.
creature	A card brought to the sorcerer's aid by a summon spell.
creature abilities	Any special effects that a creature might have as listed in the description portion of the card. Abilities can be common to many creatures or unique to one specific creature.
creature defense capacity	The ability of a card or deck to defend against creatures.
creature removal	The ability of a card or deck to remove creatures from play. This ability overlaps with damage capacity in the sense that in many cards, such as Lightning Bolts, the ability to do damage to both creatures and the opposing player is present.
damage	Wounds or damage inflicted on an opponent. Creatures cause damage when they attack, and many spells cause damage. If the damage to a creature exceeds its toughness rating, it is killed. Each point of damage done to a player results in a loss of one life point unless stated otherwise. Once a player's life points reach 0 or less, he loses the contest.

damage capacity	Everything in your deck that can inflict damage on your opponent. Most of the time, this refers to creatures and direct damage spells. In some deck configurations, it is difficult to discern the damage capacity because only combinations of cards will inflict damage.
damage prevention	The prevention or redirection of damage, the regeneration of a creature that has been assigned damage, or a creature that has been sent to the graveyard. Only the fast effects of Prevent/Redirect Damage, Regeneration, and Interrupts can be used.
damage spell percentage	The percentage of damage that instants or sorcery of a deck possess.
Dark, The	Expansion set of Magic cards based on the Dark Ages of Dominia. There are 119 unique cards in this set, and the symbol for this set is the crescent.
deck	Group of cards used to play a game of Magic. Although there is no maximum size, a deck must contain at least forty cards. Tournament play requires sixty cards.
destroyed	A card is destroyed when it is sent to the graveyard, but it may be saved by Regeneration.
Discard phase	The fifth phase of a player's turn in which the number of cards held is reduced to seven by putting extra cards in the graveyard.
Dominia	The place where Magic duels take place, often called the multiverse.
Draw phase	The third phase of a turn in which you draw one card from the top of your library. If you are unable to draw a card you have lost the duel.
duel	The process of playing an opponent in a single game of Magic.
Duelist, The	The official magazine for Magic published by Wizards of the Coast. This magazine is dedicated to Magic and other collectible trading card games.

enchantment	One of the basic Magic spell types. Enchantments are permanent until they are destroyed or the card that they are enchanting is destroyed. This type of card can only be cast during the Main phase. Other types of enchants are Enchant Land, Enchant Artifact, Enchant Creature, Enchant Wall, and Enchant World. The term "enchant" is often used in place of enchantment.
enchantment removal capacity	The ability of a deck to remove enchantments from play.
End phase	The sixth phase of a turn, in which you inform your opponent that you are finished with your turn.
environment	All of the restrictions that certain enchantments and artifacts place upon both players; for example, the Meekstone, Abyss, and Energy Flux.
evasion abilities	A creature's abilities, such as flying and landwalking, that prevent it from being blocked during the Attack phase.
Expansion Set	A limited edition set of Magic cards, 90 to 310, that were printed with a black border. The current expansion sets are Arabian Nights, Antiquities, Legends, The Dark, Fallen Empires, and Ice Age.
fast deck	A deck designed simply to kill an opponent as quickly as possible, usually sacrificing versatility for speed.
fast effect	Instants, interrupts, and abilities of permanents that are not continuous. Fast effects can be played at any time except during the Damage Healing phase.
first strike	A special ability of some creatures that allows the attacker to inflict damage before an opponent's creature can.
flying	A creature that has flying ability and cannot be blocked by a non-flying creature.
forestwalk	A creature that cannot be blocked if the defender has forests in play.
gold	Cards with a multi-colored gold border and a casting cost of more than one color of mana.
graveyard	The area where cards are sent when they are discarded, killed, used, or otherwise taken from play. This is called the discard pile.

green	One of the five colors of Magic that represents life and peace. Green gets its power from forests, and its traditional enemies are blue and black magic.
hand	Cards that a player has drawn from his or her library that have not yet been played. When cards are in your hand, they do not do anything, but they become spells when you cast them and may become creatures, artifacts, or enchantments if the casting is successful.
hand destruction deck	A deck designed to destroy your opponent's options by removing cards from his or her hand.
Heal Creatures phase	The seventh and final phase of a player's turn in which all damage to creatures is healed.
Hippy	Jargon for Hypnotic Specter.
Ice Age	The sixth Magic card expansion set.
instant	One of the basic spell types which wears off at the end of your turn. It can be played by either player and discarded once played. Special abilities are also instants for purpose of timing. Instants can also be played during the Attack phase.
intelligence	A deck's ability to obtain information about an opponent's unseen cards.
interrupt	One of the basic spell types that can be cast at any time and is the only way that a fast effect can be countered. It can be played by either player and discarded once played. Your opponent can cast more than one interrupt.
islandwalk	A creature that cannot be blocked if the defender has islands in play.
kill	To remove a creature from play and place it in the graveyard. This death can be prevented by Regeneration unless stated otherwise on the card.
land	A special card type that can only be played during the Main phase and only once per turn. All cards that are not lands are considered to be spells until they are successfully cast.
landwalk	The invasion abilities of cards such as swampwalk, mountainwalk, etc.

land destruction capacity	The ability to eliminate an opponent's lands.
land destruction deck	A deck that removes your opponent's ability to cast spells by destroying his or her mana-producing land.
Legends	The third Magic card expansion set, which has gold borders. There are approximately 300 cards in this set, released June 13, 1994. These cards require more than one type of mana to cast. Only one of each Legend card may be in play at a time.
library	The pile of cards you draw from in the Draw phase. If you run out of cards when it is your turn to draw, you lose the contest.
life points	A total of twenty points given to each player at the start of a game. Each point of damage received subtracts one life point.
life giving capacity	The ability of a card or deck to add to your total life points.
main phase	The fourth phase of a player's turn in which players cast spells (sorceries and enchantments), play one land card, and/or attack once with creatures.
mana	A term that represents magical energy that is required to cast spells and cause special effects. A common source of mana is tapping lands.
mana burn	The damage a player takes from unspent mana at the end of any phase or an Attack phase. Each point of unspent mana causes one point of colorless damage.
mana capacity	The percentage of mana in a deck.
mana pool	The total amount of mana that you have available at any given time. You take mana burn if you have mana left at the end of any phase or an Attack phase.
mountainwalk	A creature that cannot be blocked if the defender has mountains in play.
offensive creature capacity	Ability of a deck to utilize creatures for damaging the opponent.
owner	The real owner of a card as opposed to the player who might control a card at any given point in the game.
permanent	Any card that remains in play after being used, such as lands, artifacts, enchantments, and creatures.

phase	A term used to denote the seven stages of a Magic game, namely the Untap, Upkeep, Draw, Main, Discard, End, and Heal Creatures phases.
plainswalk	A creature card that cannot be blocked if the defender has plains cards in play.
pocket	Group of four cards which is the standard unit of deck construction.
poison	A creature that has the ability to poison a player when inflicting damage. If a player acquires 10 or more poison counters, he or she loses the game. Poison was introduced in the Legends expansion card set.
power	The amount of damage a creature can inflict during a normal attack. This number is the first number located in the bottom right corner of the card.
protection	A creature that has protection from a color and therefore cannot be damaged, blocked, or targeted by other cards or effects of that color. The creature may be affected by other non-damaging, non-targeting effects.
pulling a Steve	When a player tries to bend the words of a card into obscure connotations in order to create as many arguments as conceivably possible.
rampage	For each defender who has a defense of greater than one, any attacking creature with rampage gains +X/+X until end of turn. This ability was introduced in the Legends expansion card set.
red	One of the five colors of Magic that represents destruction, earth and fire, chaos and war. Red gets its power from mountains, and its traditional enemies are white and blue magic.
regeneration	The process of preventing cards from going to the graveyard by using a spell or ability. The regenerated card returns to play tapped and undamaged.
removed from game	A few spells that can cause a card to be completely removed from the game. This card is set aside and cannot be reshuffled back into your deck until the duel is over.

restricted list	A list of cards that have restrictions placed on them during convocation tournaments. Any single player cannot play more than one of these cards in a single deck.
Revised Edition	The current standard set of Magic cards which can be purchased in Starter Decks and Booster Packs.
sacrifice	When a card calls for a sacrifice, you must choose an appropriate card in play and send it to your graveyard. The card is considered buried and cannot be regenerated. If the card is under your opponent's control or it is leaving play, it cannot be placed in the graveyard.
sideboard	A term used in tournament play that consists of an extra set of fifteen cards used to fine-tune your deck.
sorcery	One of the basic spell types that takes effect immediately after being cast and may only be cast during a player's turn in the Main phase. The card is then placed in the graveyard.
source	Refers to the source of damage, creature or card. Damage is the same color as its source.
special ability	Refers to creatures that have special abilities beyond those of normal creatures. Some common abilities are banding, flying, first strike, protection, trample, rampage, and walking.
speed mana	Cards that speed up the development of a deck by increasing the amount of mana that a player has early in the game. This is important because you can only play one land per turn. In some cases, it might mean the difference in casting a large creature like a Vampire on a second turn instead of a later turn. The classic examples of speed mana are the Moxes, the Lotus, and the Sol Ring. Each of these cards is very powerful since all except the Sol Ring are out of print.
spells	There are six basic spell types: Artifact, Enchant, Instant, Interrupt, Sorcery, and Summon.
Starter Deck	Refers to a pack of sixty Magic cards, which is enough to play a tournament. Although there are no guarantees, most decks will have two rares, thirteen uncommons, and forty-five common cards.

summon	One of the basic spell types which brings a creature into play by a summoning spell during the Main phase.
summoning sickness	The state of a creature in the first turn it is summoned.
swampwalk	A creature that cannot be blocked if the defender has swamps in play.
tap	The act of marking a card by turning it sideways or putting a marker on it. Tapping a card does not generate the effect.
tapped	When a card has been turned sideways it is tapped. Artifacts that have continuous effects have no effect when tapped. Creature special effects work when tapped.
tapped out	When all of a player's mana-producing cards in play are tapped.
target	A card, token, or player toward which a spell is aimed.
territory	The area where each player plays his or her cards.
token	Any object that is used to represent a creature that was created by a spell and has no card of its own.
toughness	The amount of damage it takes to kill a creature. This is the second number in the bottom right corner of the card.
trample	A special ability that allows excess damage transfer from a blocker directly to the defending player.
trample damage	Damage done by an attacking creature with the trample special ability. This damage is applied after any normal damage is applied.
turn	A single play begins with the first game phase, Untapping cards, and ends with the seventh phase, Heal Creatures.
Unlimited Edition	A set of cards with white borders released December 1, 1993, and later replaced by the Revised Edition.
Untap phase	The first game phase, when cards are untapped at once (simultaneously).
Upkeep phase	The second game phase, where all costs (paying mana and sacrificing cards) are paid.

walk	A creature with evasion abilities such as forestwalk, islandwalk, mountainwalk, plainswalk, and swampwalk. The defender must have the appropriate card in play or the creature cannot be blocked.
wall	A special kind of creature that is not allowed to attack but is treated exactly the same as creatures.
weed	To cut out cards in a deck, thereby fine-tuning the deck.
white	One of the five colors of Magic that represents healing and protection. White gets its power from the plains, and its traditional enemies are black and red magic.
X	If a spell has an X as the costing cost, this can stand for any number of mana points as denoted on the card description.
You, Yours	Refers to the player in control or the player whose turn it is. This is usually the player who cast the spell.

Appendix A

Mana Chart and Game Player's Quick Reference

Mana Chart

Magic Type	Draw Power From	Enemies
Black	Swamps	White & Green
Blue	Islands	Red & Green
Green	Forests	Blue & Black
Red	Mountains	Blue & White
White	Plains	Red & Black

Game Phases

Phase   *Actions*

1. **Untap**
   A. Untap all of your cards in play unless existing *effects* are preventing you.
   B. Card must be tapped if tap symbol is present and its power or ability is used.
   C. You cannot play fast effects in this phase.

2. **Upkeep**
   A. Play all effects or damages (actions) as stated on each card.
   B. You can play *fast effects* during this phase.
   C. If no cards are in play for upkeep, proceed to Draw phase.

3. **Draw**
   A. Draw one card from top of your library and place in your hand.
   B. If your library is empty, you lose the duel.
   C. You can play *fast effects* during this phase.

4. **Main**
   A. Play one to three actions:
      1) Cast any type of spell except during attack.
      2) Play one land card only.
      3) Make one attack with creatures (see below for detailed attack sequences).
   B. You may cast spells or play a land card before or after the attack.
   C. During the attack, you can only play *fast effects*.
   D. You may only attack once per turn.

5. **Discard**
   A. Discard card(s) until you have seven left.
   B. *Fast effects* can be used.

6. **End**
   A. Inform your opponent that you are done for this turn.
   B. This is the last chance to use *fast effects*.

7. **Heal Creatures**
   A. Opponent can respond with *fast effects*. You can also respond.
   B. Any creature damage is erased and it is your opponent's turn.
   C. Any *fast effects* expire.

Appendix B

Card Trader's Log

Date	Card Traded	Card Traded For	Comments

Appendix B

Date	Card Traded	Card Traded For	Comments

Appendix C

A Little History

History of Magic

Magic: The Gathering™, or Magic Cards, was first released by its creator, Richard Garfield, a professor of mathematics at Whitman College in Walla Walla, Washington. Magic is a fantasy game, played with trading cards which are beautiful reproductions of paintings on 2½-by-3½-inch cards. The game requires all of the strategy of chess, the trading of baseball cards, and the deception of poker. It is a game worthy of your intellect!

Magic, one of the newest additions to the world of strategic games, has three major advantages over its predecessors. First, it is easy to learn but difficult to master. Most strategic games require a long learning period, whereas the basic rules of Magic can be learned in under an hour; however, becoming an effective player takes considerable experience and analysis. The second advantage is that a game of Magic is normally played in a relatively short period of time. Although the lengths of games are widely variable, generally games can be easily played in under half an hour. Finally, and perhaps most importantly, Magic infuses the element of trading into the game so that the concepts of the game are not static for anyone and are constantly changing and evolving.

The game was casually introduced with very conservative expectations only to be overwhelmed by an unexpected, yet welcomed, response of enthusiasm. The game has literally captured the imaginations of thousands and taken on a life of its own. Although the objective of Magic is deceptively simple, "to beat your opponent with your carefully constructed deck of cards," the game itself is as complex as one wishes to make it. People of all ages can enjoy the game, as it can be played at any degree of difficulty. Some people simply shuffle all their cards together and play, and some spend weeks honing their thousands of cards down to a sixty-card deck.

Magic is patterned after the game *Cosmic Encounter*, published by Eon Products and later marketed by Mayfair Games. Like Magic, Cosmic Encounter contains an almost limitless variety of alien interactions (or game combinations). Fascinated by how marbles were played in elementary school and the game of Strat-o-matic™ Baseball, Richard Garfield created the game of Magic by including aspects of all of these. The first prototype of Magic consisted of 120 cards that were split randomly between two players. The object of the game was to ante a card and play (duel) until you were too bored to continue. Games could last hours or minutes. At the end of the game, both players would count the number of cards they had and the player with the most won. This was the birth of Magic.

The next stage of the game introduced decks that were independent of each other. Players would still ante cards for play but the winner would keep the cards. This allowed players who were at a lower level of investment to play with others who could afford superior cards. Most of the time, those who had better cards would win more often but lose more valuable cards when they lost. The contents of an individual player's deck were unknown before the duel took place, thereby keeping the better players from relaxing and taking things for granted. Consequently, the game took on a new level of appearance and infinite possibilities.

The second state was unsurprisingly not the final version. The final version allowed the introduction of new types of cards and new complexities. This version was fully illustrated with color pictures, both of a serious and humorous nature, thereby adding to the appeal of the game.

Now that a central part of Magic was formed, the key to victory was the construction of winning decks and the effective playing of them. Early playtesters constructed the most effective decks that they could muster. They made everything they could from small creature swarm decks to land destruction decks.

Finally, the creators feared that the game might become stale and lack cohesion, and that the ability of the game system to hold together without falling into chaos would be seriously compromised. To solve this problem, the world of "Dominia" was conceived, an "infinite system of planes through which wizards travel in search of resources to fuel their magic." This added the aspect of role playing to the game. Players could develop fun themes for their decks such as the Elf or Giant deck. Players were also able to construct decks that reflected their own personalities.

Players in the game of Magic tend to swing through cycles of playing to win, playing for fun, collecting and trading, and back again. They find it enjoyable to make an excellent trade with someone, complete a set of cards, or design a colorful fun deck; however, there is no comparable feeling to winning a tournament: to be the best at that moment in time, to taste the sweet wine of victory. But no matter how you choose to play the game, you will always be playing against a vast number of people who purchase a vast number of cards, and there is always someone out there who is putting together the next great deck. Just think how many people there are in this country and other continents around the world. The numbers are staggering, and the percentage of them who are playing Magic is growing at a very rapid rate.

One final item deserves mentioning. It is hard to invent a general purpose game that can be played by all age groups and offers the participants an adequate level of challenge. Take the game of chess, for example, with its simple but elegant moves. Although there are not an infinite number of move combinations, there are enough different types of moves to make the game challenging for all levels of expertise. The game of Magic offers its players an almost limitless playing field composed of fantasy terms and mathematical combinations which can remain exciting as long as people remain creative.

Now that Magic has progressed with time, it is not uncommon for many players to come into contact with cards they have never seen before. Eventually, the game will evolve to a point where the pool of cards in existence is so large it will be too difficult to be familiar with all of them. After the printing of The Dark, there existed over 900 cards, and nearly no one can claim to own all of them. Many of the veteran addicts are familiar with each and every card and can recite their name, abilities, casting cost, and color with no reference to aid them; however, whether they will be able to keep up with the growing pool of cards remains to be seen.

Brief History of Games

As far back as 700 years ago, around the year 1282, King Alfonso X commissioned a ninety-eight-page book in his Castile of Len, Spain, entitled *Alfonso the Learned* in which he described four types of games: chess, dicing games, backgammon, and miscellaneous board games such as Alquerque or Fanorama (an elaborate capture game). His motivation for the book was to create a pastime to bring people who had fallen into another's power (slaves, seafarers, etc.) comfort and to dispel boredom so they could enjoy themselves in private. The first book of indoor games was written in English in 1674 by Charles Cotton and entitled *The Nicker Nicked: Or the Cheate of Gaming Discovered* in which he states in the opening chapter, "Gaming is an enchanting witchery, gotten betwixt Idleness and Avarice, ...an itching Disease, that makes some scratch the head, whilst others, as if they were bitten by a Tarantula, are laughing themselves to death." Games for many years were associated with such things as marked cards, cards up the sleeve, loaded dice, Russian roulette, drinking, cigars, ladies of the night, and crowded smoky rooms. Today, games are a normal part of any society, to be played for fun and enjoyment.

The real father of game books was Edmond Hoyle, a barrister who made a living at tutoring Whist to influential English people. His original intent was not to write a book on games but rather to help people improve their games by presenting laws and rules "whereby a Beginner may...attain to the Playing it well."

Today, there are literally thousands of games of all kinds to play. Magic has the promise of becoming one of the greatest strategy role-playing games of all times. And isn't it ironic that the future of this, like any game, depends upon the granddaddy of all games: *economics*. The competitive free marketplace will surely play an active role in shaping Magic and games of the future.

Appendix D

Types of Playing Environments

A Magic player can be classified into one of two environments: wild and structured.

In the *wild* environment, players duel and trade casually and can play with any source (or order) of cards. Card decks can be prearranged to form the best winning combinations versus randomly shuffling the cards. The object of this type of play is to learn how to play different deck concepts and ideas without the real pressure of dueling. Most players in the wild environment are more interested in deck building than in any other aspect of the game. Since one of the joys of the game is getting your first deck to solidly (or just) defeat an opponent, most new players to the game prefer this method of play. But this is only soothsay; you might enter the world of Dominia with a completely different approach. The choice is surely yours, my friend!

The *structured* player is a different sort of mortal altogether. This player has probably developed some high-powered winning decks and fine-tuned his or her dueling strategies to a fine glossy shine. This player takes on a more serious attitude toward winning, and the total playing field narrows to opponents of the same ability. This person takes the game very seriously and will not tolerate any loose rules or fuzzy game interpretations. This means that access to players' cards are more rigidly controlled. Decks are shuffled and each player is given a random starting deck, which could be a factory deck or a deck provided by another player. Other methods of selecting cards can be employed, but the end result is to establish a highly structured environment in which to play a game of Magic. You may wish to mark cards, have a single player keep the cards, or record the contents of all decks. Whatever method you choose, make sure that the rules are agreed on up front by all players. There is no place in Dominia for those foolish enough to intentionally deceive others!

Appendix E

Cards Removed from Original Edition

This is a list of cards which have been removed and banned from play due to the unfair advantage they give an individual player. It might noted that there are two other lists of cards that should be reviewed before regular or tournament play: the Restricted list and the Banned list. These are subject to change.

These cards were removed because they were too confusing, created too many paradox situations, or violated basic game rules:

Blaze of Glory
Illusionary Mask
Jade Statue
Lich
Raging River
Twiddle
Two-Headed Giant of Forys
Word of Command

These cards were removed because they tended to cause an imbalance in game play. Most of them are on the Restricted or Banned lists:

Ancestral Recall
Berserk
Black Lotus
Forcefield

Gauntlet of Might
Ice Storm
Mox Emerald
Mox Jet
Mox Ruby
Mox Sapphire
Sinkhole
Time Vault
Timetwister
Timewalk

These cards were removed to make room for new cards from the Arabian Nights and Antiquities sets:

Chaos Orb
Consecrate Land
Copper Tablet
Cyclopean Tomb
Dwarven Demolition Team
False Orders
Icy Manipulator
Invisibility
Ironclaw Orcs
Natural Selection
Psionic Blast

Appendix F

Magic on the Net

A wealth of information about Magic: The Gathering™ is available from the Internet web pages. Access this information by entering the following URL to display the Magic home page:

http://marvin.macc.wisc.edu:80/deckmaster/magic

Go to the bottom of the page and select the More Magic on the Net icon to display a list of all Magic web pages and obtain the latest up-to-date information on Magic: The Gathering and other related topics.

Click on the blue text to bring up the home page you are interested in, such as information about players, clubs, card trading auctions, news groups, product support, card descriptions, rulings, strategies, tournaments, etc.

Appendix G

Errors and General Corrections on Magic Cards

The following is a list of all known "Error cards" in Magic: The Gathering™. These errors consist of misprints, undesirable wordings, and cards that require clarification or further corrections.

Something happens...graveyard:
Cards that say "something happens if a card goes to the graveyard." This should be reworded to say that "the effect only occurs if it goes to the graveyard from play."

Card cannot be used...summons:
A card that cannot be used against creatures summoned this turn should instead be played as if it cannot be used against creatures which entered the controller's territory. The following cards are affected: *Onulet* (AQ, RV), *Personal Incarnation* (A, B, UL, RV), *Rukh Egg* (AN), and *Su-Chi* (AQ).

Any card...discarding:
A card that specifies "discarding" something in play should instead say "destroyed."

Any card...destroys itself:
Any card that specifies that it destroys itself when it is used should be played as a sacrifice (part of the cost).

Alpha printing...the correct artist:
In the Alpha printing, a number of cards incorrectly specified the artist. The following cards are affected: *Circle of Protection: Red* (Mark Tedin), *Death Ward* (Mark Poole), *Sedge Troll* (Dan Frazier), and *Tropical Island* (Jesper Myrfors).

Shuler should be Schuler for artwork:
Douglas Shuler's name should be "Schuler" wherever artwork is specified.

Mana symbols representing colors:
Some cards were printed with mana symbols representing the various mana colors (B, U, G, R, and W for black, blue, green, red, and white). The following cards are affected: *Demonic Hordes, Drain Life, Force of Nature, Phantasmal Forces*, and *Rick Hydra*.

Arabian Nights Expansion Set...shouldn't have mountain:
In the Arabian Nights Expansion Set, the incorrect Mountian card should be a Desert.

Dark card set...incorrect artwork artists:
In the Dark card set, the artist's name Denise Detwiler should be Dennis Detwiller.

Legends Expansion Set...incorrect artwork artists:
In the Legends Expansion Set, the following correct artwork artists should be specified: *Active Volcano*—Justin Hampton, *Disharmony*—Byron Wackwitz, *Psionic Entity*—Justin Hampton.

All Hallow's Eve cards...should be sorcery:
In all *Hallow's Eve* cards, the type is a sorcery instead of an enchantment.

Ball Lightning card...is destroyed:
In the *Ball Lightning* card, the phrase "...is destroyed at the end of the turn in which it is summoned" should be changed to "...is destroyed at the end of the turn in which it is brought into play."

Basalt Monolith card...mana generated and mana symbol missing:
Mana generated by any *Basalt Monolith* or *Mana Vault* cannot be used to untap any *Basalt Monolith* or *Mana Vault*. This ruling by Wizards of the Coast prevents powerful card combinations from being played that are unfair. Also, on the *Basalt Monolith* card, the mana symbol in the text was omitted. The text should be "spend 3 to untap."

Birds of Paradise card...two slashes:
On the *Birds of Paradise* card, there should only be one slash between the power and toughness values.

Blood Lust card...target creature:
On the *Blood Lust* card, the text should read "Target creature..." instead of "Target creatures...."

Channel card...text:
On the *Channel* card, the text wording in the first sentence was changed from "...for 1 life each" to "...at a cost of 1 life each," and the last sentence was changed from "Life spent this way is not considered damage" to "Effects that prevent damage may not be used to counter this loss of life." The change described in the *Pocket Player's Guide* on page 190 was incorrect.

Cocoon card...play card:
You should play the *Cocoon* card as if it says "Tap target creature that you control and put three counters on Cocoon."

Cyclopean Tomb card...casting cost omitted:
On the *Cyclopean Tomb* card, the casting cost of "4" was omitted.

Circle of Protection: Black...cards omitted:
The card *Circle of Protection: Black* was omitted from the Alpha printing plates.

Conservator card...loss of life:
The text of the *Conservator* card should read and be played as follows: "3 Tap: Prevent up to 2 damage to any player." The confusion is that most cards that refer to "loss of life" should really refer to "damage."

Disintegrate card..omitted regenerated:
On the *Disintegrate* card, the words "and cannot be regenerated" were omitted.

Eater of the Dead card...remove creature:
The following text should be added to the *Eater of the Dead*: "This ability can only be used if the *Eater of the Dead* is tapped."

Appendix G

Elvish Archers card...wrong P/T:
The power/toughness values for the *Elvish Archers* card was switched from
to 2/1.

Firestorm Phoenix card...ignore word:
On the *Firestorm Phoenix* card, ignore the word "instead" in "...return it to
the owner's hand instead."

Forcefield card...text:
The text of the *Forcefield* card should read and be played as follows:
"1: Prevent all but 1 damage from an unblocked attacker." The error in
the errata printing in *The Duelist* #2 was accidentally copied from the
Conservator below it.

Gaea's Touch card...text alignment:
The text in the *Gaea's Touch* card is incorrectly shifted to the left with no
left margin, leaving an extra wide right margin.

Icy Manipulator card...helpful reminder that doesn't help:
The helpful reminder "No Effects are generated by the target card" on the
Icy Manipulator card caused more confusion than the original wording. As
a consequence, the card was removed from the Revised Edition.

Imprison card...gray circle misplaced:
On the *Imprison* card, the gray circle is misplaced above the cost and
should be behind the "1".

Island Sanctuary card...creature attack:
On the *Island Sanctuary* card, the phrase "the only creatures that may
damage you" was changed to "the only creatures that may attack you."

Karma card...damage:
In the text of the *Karma* card, "...Karma does 1 damage to the swamp
owner during his or her upkeep" was changed to "...Karma does 1 damage
to the swamp owner during the swamp owner's upkeep."

Knowledge Vault card...what if stolen:
On the *Knowledge Vault* card, add the the text: "If Knowledge Vault leaves
play or your control, place all cards under it in the graveyard."

Living Artifact card...text:
The text of the *Living Artifact* card should read and be played as follows: "Put a counter on Living Artifact for each damage done to you." This is another change from "loss of life."

Mana Short card...add sentence:
The following sentence was added to the *Mana Short* card: "Opponent takes no damage from unspent mana.

Nightmare card...misprint:
On the *Nightmare* card, the word "swamp" in the card text was flawed.

Orcish Oriflamme card..casting cost:
On the *Orcish Oriflamme* card, the casting cost was changed from 1R to 3R.

Onulet card...incorrect artist:
The incorrect artist on the *Onulet* card was specified; the correct artist is Anson Maddocks.

Reconstruction card...expansion symbol omitted:
On the *Reconstruction* card, the Anvil expansion symbol was omitted.

Red Elemental Blast card...wrong type:
The *Red Elemental Blast* card is an Interrupt and not an Instant as specified on the card.

Relic Bind card...too powerful:
Wizards of the Coast has decided that the *Relic Bind* card is too powerful. If played, then the text should read: "When target artifact that opponent controls is tapped...."

Runesword card...flawed printing:
Some of the *Runesword* cards were accidentally printed with a large black line running diagonally in the text box. The line has no meaning.

Serendib Efreet card...incorrect border:
The *Serendib Efreet* is a blue card but has an incorrect green border. The artwork is incorrectly specified from the Arabian Nights *Ifh-Bif Efreet* card.

Twiddle card...helplful reminder:
On the *Twiddle* card, the helpful reminder that was also added to the *Icy Manipulator* card was added here.

Unsummon card...text:
The *Unsummon* card text should read "...enchantments on creature are discarded" instead of "...enchantments on creature are CARDed."

Venarian Gold...card...X counters:
The *Venarian Gold* card should be played as if it says "Put X counters on Venarian Gold" instead of "Put X counters on target creature."

Volcanic Island...card omitted:
The card *Volcanic Island* was omitted from the Alpha printing plates.

White Ward card...add text:
Since the *White Ward* card should remove itself from a creature it is placed on, the following text should be added onto the end: "The protection granted by White Ward will not cause itself to be destroyed."

Appendix H

Beginner's Magic Card Reference

Revised Edition Only

Note: Beige and brown colors also denote land and artifact cards.

[1] — In Type I tournaments, only one of this card (including the sideboard) may be played.

[2] — Banned from Type I tournament play.

[3] — In Type II tournaments, only one of this card (including the sideboard) may be played.

[4] — Banned from Type II tournament play.

Legend

Cost:	B = Black, G = Green, R = Red, W = White, U = Blue, # = Colorless
Power/Toughness:	Power/Toughness rating = value 1-10; * = determined by the description portion of card

Card Name	Card Type	Color	Casting Cost	Power/ Toughness	Text
A					
Air Elemental	Summon Elemental	Blue	3UU	4/4	Flying
Aladdin's Lamp	Artifact	Brown	10	–	Instead of drawing in draw phase, draw X cards and keep only one (X,T).
Aladdin's Ring	Artifact	Brown	8	–	Damage to any target (8,T).

Card Name	Card Type	Color	Casting Cost	Power/ Toughness	Text
Animate Artifact	Enchant Artifact	Blue	3U	--	Makes target artifact a */* creature where * = casting cost; no effect on artifact creatures.
Animate Dead	Enchant Creature	Black	1B	--	Pull creature from any graveyard at -1 power.
Animate Wall	Enchant Wall	White	W	--	Target wall can attack.
Ankh of Mishra	Artifact	Brown	2	--	2 damage to anyone who plays a hand.
Armageddon	Sorcery	White	3W	--	Destroys all lands in play.
Armageddon Clock	Artifact	Brown	6	--	Add one counter each upkeep; does 1 damage to all players for each token at end of upkeep; any player may remove a token for 4 mana.
Aspect of Wolf	Enchant Creature	Green	G	--	Gives +*/+* where * = 1/2 number of forests (round down power and up toughness).
Atog	Summon Atog	Red	1R	1/2	+2/+0 until end of turn if sacrifice artifact.
B					
Bad Moon	Enchantment	Black	1B	--	Gives +1/+1 to all black creatures.
Badlands	Land	Beige	--	--	Tap for 1 black or red mana.
Balance	Sorcery	White	1W	--	Balance number of creatures, lands, and cards in play.
Basalt Monolith	Artifact	Brown	3	--	Tap to get 3 mana; untap by spending 3 mana.
Bayou	Land	Beige	--	--	Tap for 1 black or green mana.
Benalish Hero	Summon Hero	White	W	1/1	Bands
Birds of Paradise	Summon Mana Birds	Green	G	0/1	Flying; tap for one mana of any color.
Black Knight	Summon Knight	Black	BB	2/2	First strike; protection from white.
Black Vise	Artifact	Brown	1	--	1 damage during upkeep to opponent for each card over 4 in hand.
Black Ward	Enchant Artifact	White	W	--	Gives protection from black.
Blessing	Enchant Creature	White	WW	--	+1/+1 (W)
Blue Elemental Blast	Interrupt	Blue	U	--	Destroys red card or counters red spell.

Card Name	Card Type	Color	Casting Cost	Power/ Toughness	Text
Blue Ward	Enchant Creature	White	W	---	Gives protection from blue.
Bog Wraith	Summon Wraith	Black	3B	3/3	Swampalk
Bottle of Suleiman	Artifact	Brown	5	---	Flip coin and take 5 damage or get 5/5 Flying Djinn token creature (1,T); Bottle destroyed when used.
Braingeyser[1, 3]	Sorcery	Blue	XUU	---	Draw (or force opponent) X cards.
Brass Man	Artifact-Creature	Brown	1	1/3	Pay 1 to untap during upkeep.
Burrowing	Enchant Creature	Red	R	---	Gives mountainwalk.
C					
Castle	Enchantment	White	3W	---	Untapped (non-attacking) creatures gain +2/+2.
Celestial Prism	Artifact	Brown	3	---	1 mana of any color (2,T).
Channel[1, 3]	Sorcery	Green	GG	---	Turn life into colorless mana for rest of turn.
Chaoslace	Interrupt	Red	R	---	Change one card color to red.
Circle of Protection: Black	Enchantment	White	1W	---	Prevent all damage against you from only one black source (1,T). Pay 1 mana each time you prevent damage if source does damage to you more than once in a turn.
Circle of Protection: Blue	Enchantment	White	1W	---	Prevent all damage against you from only one blue source (1,T). Pay 1 mana each time you prevent damage if source does damage to you more than once in a turn.
Circle of Protection: Green	Enchantment	White	1W	---	Prevent all damage against you from only one green source (1,T). Pay 1 mana each time you prevent damage if source does damage to you more than once in a turn.
Circle of Protection: Red	Enchantment	White	1W	---	Prevent all damage against you from only one red source (1,T). Pay 1 mana each time you prevent damage if source does damage to you more than once in a turn.
Circle of Protection: White	Enchantment	White	1W	---	Prevent all damage against you from only one white source (1,T). Pay 1 mana each time you prevent damage if source does damage to you more than once in a turn.

Card Name	Card Type	Color	Casting Cost	Power/ Toughness	Text
Clockwork Beast	Artifact-Creature	Brown	6	0/4	Starts with 7 +1/+0 tokens; uses token when attacking or defending; do not untap to pay 1 mana per token restored (taps if wasn't already).
Clone	Summon Clone	Blue	3U	*/*	Where * = copies creature and color.
Cockatrice	Summon Cockatrice	Green	3GG	2/4	Flying; any non-wall blocked-by/blocking it is destroyed.
Conservator	Artifact	Brown	4	–	Prevent loss of up to 2 life (3,T).
Contract from Below[2, 4]	Sorcery	Black	B	–	Get new hand but add one card to ante.
Control Magic	Enchant Creature	Blue	2UU	–	Caster takes control of target creature.
Conversion	Enchantment	White	2WW	–	All mountains become plains; costs WW during upkeep.
Copy Artifact[1, 3]	Enchantment	Blue	1U	–	Card acts as a copy of an artifact in play.
Counterspell	Interrupt	Blue	UU	–	Counters spell as being cast.
Craw Wurm	Summon Wurm	Green	4GG	6/4	
Creature Bond	Enchant Creature	Blue	1U	–	Creature Bond does damage to controller when creature goes to graveyard.
Crumble	Instant	Green	G	–	Buries target artifact and gives controller life equal to its casting cost.
Crusade	Enchantment	White	WW	–	+1/+1 to all white creatures.
Crystal Rod	Artifact	Brown	1	–	+1 life when blue spell is cast (1).
Cursed Land	Enchant Land	Black	2BB	–	1 damage; must discard down to 4 cards during discard.
D					
Dancing Scimitar	Artifact-Creature	Brown	4	1/5	Flying
Dark Ritual	Interrupt	Black	B	–	Add 3 black mana to mana pool.
Darkpact[2, 4]	Sorcery	Black	BBB	–	Swap top card of library with either ante.
Death Ward	Instant	White	W	–	Regenerates creature.
Deathgrip	Enchantment	Black	BB	–	Counter green spell as it is cast (BB).

Card Name	Card Type	Color	Casting Cost	Power/ Toughness	Text
Deathlace	Interrupt	Black	B	--	Change one card color to black.
Demonic Attorney[2, 4]	Sorcery	Black	1B	--	All players ante another card or forfeit.
Demonic Hordes	Summon Demons	Black	3BBB	5/5	Tap to destroy a land; BBB upkeep or lose a land and it becomes tapped.
Demonic Tutor[1, 3]	Sorcery	Black	1B	--	Take any one card from library into hand.
Desert Twister	Sorcery	Green	4GG	--	Destroy any 1 card in play.
Dingus Egg	Artifact	Brown	4	--	2 damage to controller of any land which is destroyed.
Disenchant	Instant	White	1W	--	Destroy enchantment or artifact.
Disintegrate	Sorcery	Red	XR	--	X damage to target; cannot regenerate this turn; leaves game if it dies this turn.
Disrupting Scepter	Artifact	Brown	3	--	Opponent discards one card (3,T).
Dragon Engine	Artifact-Creature	Brown	3	1/3	+1/+0 (2)
Dragon Whelp	Summon Dragon	Red	2RR	2/3	Flying; +1/+0 (R); dies at end of turn if more than RRR spent in one turn.
Drain Life	Sorcery	Black	1B	--	X damage to target; +X life to caster (X is black).
Drain Power	Sorcery	Blue	UU	--	Tap all of opponent's land; add opponent's mana pool to your pool.
Drudge Skeletons	Summon Skeletons	Black	1B	1/1	Regenerates (B)
Dwarven Warriors	Summon Dwarves	Red	2R	1/1	Tap to make power <3 creature unblockable.
Dwarven Weaponsmith	Summon Dwarves	Red	1R	1/1	Tap and sacrifice artifact during upkeep to give a permanent +1/+1 to target creature.
E					
Earth Elemental	Summon Elemental	Red	3RR	4/5	
Earthbind	Enchant Creature	Red	R	--	2 damage to creature; loses flying; does not affect non-flying creatures (not cardable on them).
Earthquake	Sorcery	Red	XR	--	All players and non-flying creatures take X damage.

Card Name	Card Type	Color	Casting Cost	Power/ Toughness	Text
Ebony Horse	Artifact	Brown	3	--	Attacking creatures escape after defense is chosen (2,T).
El-Hajjaj	Summon El-Hajjaj	Black	1BB	1/1	+1 life for each damage he does to any target.
Elvish Archers	Summon Elves	Green	1G	2/1	First strike
Energy Flux	Enchantment	Blue	2U	--	Pay 2 for each artifact during upkeep or it is destroyed.
Erg Raiders	Summon Raiders	Black	1B	2/3	Take 2 damage if you do not attack each turn.
Evil Presence	Enchant Land	Black	B	--	Target land is now swamp.
Eye for an Eye	Instant	White	WW	--	Opponent takes damage equal to that inflicted on you by your opponent's spells or creatures.
F					
Farmstead	Enchant Land	White	WWW	--	+1 life during upkeep (WW) once per turn.
Fastbond	Enchantment	Green	G	--	Can play extra lands for 1 damage each.
Fear	Enchant Creature	Black	BB	--	Only blockable by black or artifact creatures.
Feedback	Enchant Enchantment	Blue	2U	--	1 damage to controller during upkeep.
Fire Elemental	Summon Elemental	Red	3RR	5/4	
Fireball	Sorcery	Red	XR	--	X damage to target; each extra target (1); split damage evenly.
Firebreathing	Enchant Creature	Red	R	--	Gives +1/+0 (R)
Flashfires	Sorcery	Red	3R	--	Destroys all plains.
Flight	Enchant Creature	Blue	U	--	Gives flying
Flying Carpet	Artifact	Brown	4	--	Gives flying until end of turn (2,T); destroyed if creature destroyed when using it.
Fog	Instant	Green	G	--	No damage or other effects from this attack.
Force of Nature	Summon Force	Green	2GGGG	8/8	Trample; costs GGGG during upkeep or take 8 damage.
Forest - Big Tree	Land	Green	--	--	Tap for 1 green mana.

Card Name	Card Type	Color	Casting Cost	Power/ Toughness	Text
Forest - Path	Land	Green	--	--	Tap for 1 green mana.
Forest - Shadows	Land	Green	--	--	Tap for 1 green mana.
Fork	Interrupt	Red	RR	--	Copy Sorcery or Instant and control the duplicate.
Frozen Shade	Summon Shade	Black	2B	0/1	B: +1/+1
Fungusaur	Summon Fungusaur	Green	3G	2/2	Gets +1/+1 token when damaged and not killed.
G					
Gaea's Liege	Summon Gaea's Liege	Green	3GGG	*/*	Where * = number of forests of opponent when attacking.
Giant Growth	Instant	Green	G	--	+3/+3 to creature until end of turn.
Giant Spider	Summon Spider	Green	3G	2/4	Can block flying creatures.
Glasses of Urza	Artifact	Brown	1	--	Tap to look at one opponent's hand.
Gloom	Enchantment	Black	2B	--	White spells and white enchantments cost 3 more (was white spells and circles of protection).
Goblin Balloon Brigade	Summon Goblins	Red	R	1/1	Flying (R)
Goblin King	Summon Goblin King	Red	1RR	2/2	All goblins get +1/+1 and mountainwalk.
Granite Gargoyle	Summon Gargoyle	Red	2R	2/2	Flying; +0/+1 (R)
Gray Ogre	Summon Ogre	Red	2R	2/2	
Green Ward	Enchant Creature	White	W	--	Gives protection from green.
Grizzly Bears	Summon Bears	Green	1G	2/2	
Guardian Angel	Instant	White	XW	--	Prevents X damage to target; can pay to prevent further damage to the target this turn.
H					
Healing Salve	Instant	White	W	--	+3 life or prevent 3 damage.
Helm of Chatzuk	Artifact	Brown	1	--	Give creature banding until end of turn (1,T).
Hill Giant	Summon Giant	Red	3R	3/3	
The Hive	Artifact	Brown	5	--	Make 1/1 flying wasp (5,T).

Card Name	Card Type	Color	Casting Cost	Power/ Toughness	Text
Holy Armor	Enchant Creature	White	W	--	Gains +0/+2; (W): +0/+1.
Holy Strength	Enchant Creature	White	W	--	Gains +1/+2
Howl from Beyond	Instant	Black	XB	--	+X/+0 until end of turn.
Howling Mine	Artifact	Brown	2	--	All players draw 1 extra card during Draw phase.
Hurkyl's Recall	Instant	Blue	U	--	Sends all of target player's artifacts from play into land.
Hurloon Minotaur	Summon Minotaur	Red	1RR	2/3	
Hurricane	Sorcery	Green	XG	--	All players and flying creatures take X damage.
Hypnotic Specter	Summon Specter	Black	1BB	2/2	Flying; player discards if damaged by specter.
I					
Instill Energy	Enchant Creature	Green	G	--	May untap once during your turn in addition to the untap phase; may attack on turn it enters play.
Iron Star	Poly Artifact	Brown	1	--	+1 life when red spell cast (1).
Ironroot Treefolk	Summon Treefolk	Green	4G	3/5	
Island - Greenish	Land	Blue	--	--	Tap for 1 blue mana.
Island - Purplish	Land	Blue	--	--	Tap for 1 blue mana.
Island - Red Sky	Land	Blue	--	--	Tap for 1 blue mana.
Island Fish Jasconius	Summon Island Fish	Blue	4UUU	6/8	Pay UUU to untap during upkeep; cannot attack if opponent does not have islands; destroyed if you have no islands.
Island Sanctuary	Enchantment	White	1W	--	You don't have to draw a card from library; only creatures that can attack you until next turn are ones that fly or have islandwalk.
Ivory Cup	Artifact	Brown	1	--	+1 life when white spell cast (1).
Ivory Tower[1, 3]	Artifact	Brown	1	--	+1 life for each card over 4 in hand at beginning of turn.
J					
Jade Monolith	Artifact	Brown	4	--	Transfer damage to self from creature (1).

Card Name	Card Type	Color	Casting Cost	Power/ Toughness	Text
Jandor's Ring	Artifact	Brown	6	--	Discard the card just drawn and replace it (2,T).
Jandor's Saddlebags	Artifact	Brown	2	--	Untap a creature (3,T).
Jayemdae Tome	Artifact	Brown	4	--	Draw a card (4,T).
Juggernaut	Artifact-Creature	Brown	4	5/3	If possible, must attack each turn; cannot be blocked by walls.
Jump	Instant	Blue	U	--	Creature is flying until end of turn.
K					
Karma	Enchantment	White	2WW	--	1 damage during upkeep for each swamp.
Keldon Warlord	Summon Lord	Red	2RR	*/*	Where * = number of non-wall creatures you have.
Kird Ape	Summon Ape	Red	R	1/1	+1/+2 if you have forests.
Kormus Bell	Artifact	Brown	4	--	All swamps become 1/1 creatures.
Kudzu	Enchant Land	Green	1GG	--	Destroys land when land is tapped then moves to another land.
L					
Lance	Enchant Creature	White	W	--	Gives first strike.
Ley Druid	Summon Cleric	Green	2G	1/1	Tap to untap land of choice.
Library of Leng	Artifact	Brown	1	--	Skip discard phase; can discard to top of library (was no limit to hand size).
Lifeforce	Enchantment	Green	GG	--	Counter black spell as cast (GG).
Lifelace	Interrupt	Green	G	--	Changes card color to green.
Lifetap	Enchantment	Blue	UU	--	+1 life when opponent taps a forest.
Lightning Bolt	Instant	Red	R	--	3 damage to one target.
Living Artifact	Enchant Artifact	Green	G	--	Put one token on artifact for each life lost; can convert one token to +1 life each upkeep.
Living Lands	Enchantment	Green	3G	--	Treat all forests in play as 1/1 creatures.
Living Wall	Artifact Creature	Brown	4	0/6	Wall; regenerates (1).
Llanowar Elves	Summon Elves	Green	G	1/1	Tap for 1 green mana.

Card Name	Card Type	Color	Casting Cost	Power/ Toughness	Text
Lord of Atlantis	Summon Lord	Blue	UU	2/2	All Merfolk get +1/+1 and islandwalk.
Lord of the Pit	Summon Demon	Black	4BBB	7/7	Trample; flying; sacrifice one creature during upkeep to take 7 damage.
Lure	Enchant Creature	Green	1GG	--	All creatures able to block target must do so.
M					
Magical Hack	Interrupt	Blue	U	--	Change land type references on one card.
Magnetic Mountain	Enchantment	Red	1RR	--	Blue creatures cost 4 to untap during upkeep.
Mahamoti Djinn	Summon Djinn	Blue	4UU	5/6	Flying
Mana Flare	Enchantment	Red	2R	--	All mana producing lands produce one extra mana.
Mana Short	Instant	Blue	2U	--	All opponent's land is tapped and pool emptied.
Mana Vault	Artifact	Brown	1	--	Tap for 3 colorless mana; untap for 4 mana during upkeep or take 1 damage.
Manabarbs	Enchantment	Red	3R	--	1 damage to anyone who taps a land.
Meekstone	Artifact	Brown	1	--	Creatures with power >2 do not untap.
Merfolk of thePearl Trident	Summon Merfolk	Blue	U	1/1	
Mesa Pegasus	Summon Pegasus	White	1W	1/1	Flying; bands.
Mijae Djinn	Summon Djinn	Red	RRR	6/3	Flip coin when attacking.
Millstone	Artifact	Brown	2	--	Opponent discards 2 cards from top of library (2,T).
Mind Twist[1, 3]	Sorcery	Black	XB	--	Opponent discards X cards at random.
Mishra's War Machine	Artifact-Creature	Brown	7	5/5	Bands; discard 1 card from hand each upkeep or take 3 damage and becomes tapped.
Mons's Goblin Raiders	Summon Goblins	Red	R	1/1	
Mountain - Blue Sky	Land	Red	--	--	Tap for 1 red mana.

Card Name	Card Type	Color	Casting Cost	Power/Toughness	Text
Mountain - GreenSky	Land	Red	--	--	Tap for 1 red mana.
Mountain - Red Sky	Land	Red	--	--	Tap for 1 red mana.
N					
Nether Shadow	Summon Shadow	Black	B	1/1	If Nether Shadow is in the graveyard and three creatures are above it, then it comes into play during the upkeep phase.
Nettling Imp	Summon Imp	Black	2B	1/1	Tap to force a non-wall to attack or die.
Nevinyrral's Disk	Artifact	Brown	4	--	Destroy all creatures, enchantments, and artifacts (1, T); begins tapped.
Nightmare	Summon Nightmare	Black	5B	*/*	Flying; * = number of swamps.
Northern Paladin	Summon Paladin	White	2WW	3/3	Destroy black card (WW,T).
O					
Obsianus Golem	Artifact-Creature	Brown	6	4/6	
Onulet	Artifact-Creature	Brown	3	2/2	Controller gets +2 life when destroyed.
Orcish Artillery	Summon Orcs	Red	1RR	1/3	Tap for 2 damage to target; 3 damage to controller.
Orcish Oriflamme	Enchantment	Red	3R	--	All attacking creatures during attack phase gain +1/+0.
Ornithopter	Artifact-Creature	Brown	0	0/2	Flying.
P					
Paralyze	Enchant Creature	Black	B	--	Taps creature; requires 4 to untap creature during upkeep.
Pearled Unicorn	Summon Unicorn	White	2W	2/2	
Personal Incarnation	Summon Avatar	White	3WWW	6/6	Can redirect damage from it to controller, lose 1/2 of life it it dies (rounding loss up).
Pestilence	Enchantment	Black	2BB	--	1 damage to creatures and players (B); discard if no creatures in play at end of turn.
Phantasmal Forces	Summon Phantasm	Blue	3U	4/1	Flying; costs U during upkeep or dies.

Card Name	Card Type	Color	Casting Cost	Power/ Toughness	Text
Phantasmal Terrain	Enchant Land	Blue	UU	--	Changes land to a basic type of your choice.
Phantom Monster	Summon Phantasm	Blue	3U	3/3	Flying
Pirate Ship	Summon Ship	Blue	4U	4/3	Tap to do 1 damage to target; opponent must have islands to attack with this card; destroyed if you have no islands.
Plague Rats	Summon Rats	Black	2B	*/*	* = number of rats in play.
Plains - Dark	Land	White	--	--	Tap for 1 white mana.
Plains - Dots	Land	White	--	--	Tap for 1 white mana.
Plains - Trees	Land	White	--	--	Tap for 1 white mana.
Plateau	Land	Beige	--	--	Tap for one red or white mana.
Power Leak	Enchant Enchantment	Blue	1U	--	Enchantment costs 2 during upkeep or take 1 damage for each unpaid mana.
Power Sink	Interrupt	Blue	XU	--	Opponent spends X mana or spell fails; if cannot, all lands are tapped.
Power Surge	Enchantment	Blue	RR	--	During upkeep phase, all players take 1 damage per land which was untapped at beginning of turn.
Primal Clay	Artifact-Creature	Brown	6	*/*	At casting, choose to make it a 3/3 creature, a 1/6 wall, or a 2/2 flying creature.
Prodigal Sorcerer	Summon Wizard	Blue	2U	1/1	Tap for 1 damage to target.
Psychic Venom	Enchant Land	Blue	1U	--	2 damage when target land is tapped.
Purelace	Interrupt	White	W	--	Change one card to white.
R					
The Rack	Artifact	Brown	1	--	Opponent takes 1 damage for each card less than 3 in hand at beginning of turn.
Raise Dead	Sorcery	Black	B	--	Return creature from graveyard to hand.
Reconstruction	Sorcery	Blue	U	--	Take artifact from your graveyard to your hand.
Red Elemental Blast	Interrupt	Red	R	--	Counters blue spell or destroys blue card.

Card Name	Card Type	Color	Casting Cost	Power/ Toughness	Text
Red Ward	Enchant Creature	White	W	--	Gives protection from red.
Regeneration	Enchant Creature	Green	1GG	--	Gives regeneration (G).
Regrowth[1, 3]	Sorcery	Green	1G	--	Return any card from graveyard to hand.
Resurrection	Sorcery	White	2WW	--	Take creature from graveyard and put into play.
Reverse Damage	Instant	White	1WW	--	All damage from one source is instead added to life.
Reverse Polarity	Instant	White	WW	--	All damage done by artifacts to you so far this turn is instead added to life.
Righteousness	Instant	White	W	--	+7/+7 to defending creature.
Roc of Kher Ridges	Summon Roc	Red	3R	3/3	Flying
Rock Hydra	Summon Hydra	Red	XRR	0/0	Starts with X +1/+1 tokens; loses 1 token for each point of damage unless R spent; pay RRR during upkeep to get new token.
Rocket Launcher	Artifact	Brown	4	--	1 damage to any target (2); goes to graveyard at end of turn in which it is used; cannot be used until your turn in play begins.
Rod of Ruin	Artifact	Brown	4	--	1 damage to any target (3,T).
Royal Assassin	Summon Assassin	Black	1BB	1/1	Tap to destroy one tapped creature.
S					
Sacrifice	Interrupt	Black	B	--	Sacrifice creature and add casting cost as black mana to pool.
Samite Healer	Summon Cleric	White	1W	1/1	Tap to prevent 1 damage to any target.
Savannah	Land	Beige	--	--	Tap for 1 green or white mana.
Savannah Lions	Summon Lions	White	W	2/1	
Scathe Zombies	Summon Zombies	Black	2B	2/2	
Scavenging Ghoul	Summon Ghoul	Black	3B	2/2	+1 token of regeneration at end of turn for each creature that dies.
Scrubland	Land	Beige	--	--	Tap for 1 black or white mana.
Scryb Sprites	Summon Faeries	Green	G	1/1	Flying

Card Name	Card Type	Color	Casting Cost	Power/ Toughness	Text
Sea Serpent	Summon Serpent	Blue	5U	5/5	Opponent must have islands to attack with this card; buried if you have no islands.
Sedge Troll	Summon Troll	Red	2R	2/2	+1/+1 if you have swamps; regenerate (B).
Sengir Vampire	Summon Vampire	Black	3BB	4/4	Flying; gets +1/+1 token when creature dies which was damaged by the vampire.
Serendib Efreet	Summon Efreet	Blue	2U	3/4	Flying; take 1 damage during upkeep.
Serra Angel	Summon Angel	White	3WW	4/4	Flying; does not tap when attacking.
Shanodin Dryads	Summon Nymphs	Green	G	1/1	Forestwalk.
Shatter	Instant	Red	R	–	Destroy one artifact.
Shatterstorm	Sorcery	Red	2RR	–	All artifacts in play are buried.
Shivan Dragon	Summon Dragon	Red	4RR	5/5	Flying; +1/+0 (R).
Simulacrum	Instant	Black	1B	–	Transfer all damage so far this turn from self to a creature.
Siren's Call	Instant	Blue	U		All non-walls of opponent attack or die.
Sleight of Mind	Interrupt	Blue	U	–	Change color type references on one card.
Smoke	Enchantment	Red	RR	–	Players may only untap one creature during untap.
Sol Ring[1,3]	Artifact	Brown	1	–	Tap for 2 colorless mana.
Sorceress Queen	Summon Sorceress	Black	1BB	1/1	Tap to make a creature 0/2 until end of turn.
Soul Net	Artifact	Brown	1	–	+1 life when creature goes to the graveyard (1).
Spell Blast	Interrupt	Blue	XU	–	Counters target spell of cost X.
Stasis	Enchantment	Blue	1U	–	No untap phase; costs U in upkeep.
Steal Artifact	Enchant Artifact	Blue	2UU	–	Takes control of artifact.
Stone Giant	Summon Giant	Red	2RR	3/4	Tap to fly other creature of toughness less than Giant's power (kills it).
Stone Rain	Sorcery	Red	2R	–	Destroy one land.
Stream of Life	Sorcery	Green	XG	–	+X life to target player.

Card Name	Card Type	Color	Casting Cost	Power/ Toughness	Text
Sunglasses of Urza	Artifact	Brown	3	--	Can use white mana as red mana.
Swamp - Brownish	Land	Black	--	--	Tap for 1 black mana.
Swamp - Greenish	Land	Black	--	--	Tap for 1 black mana.
Swamp - Whitish	Land	Black	--	--	Tap for 1 black mana.
Swords of Plowshares	Instant	White	W	--	Tap and sacrifice this card and as many of your creatures as you want to do damage to one target equal to the sum of the power of all creatures sacrificed.
T					
Taiga	Land	Beige	--	--	Tap for 1 green or red mana.
Terror	Instant	Black	1B	--	Buries non-black/Artifact creature.
Thicket Basilisk	Summon Basilisk	Green	3GG	2/4	Any non-wall blocked-by/blocking it is destroyed.
Thoughtlace	Interrupt	Blue	U	--	Change one color to blue.
Throne of Bone	Artifact	Brown	1	--	+1 life when black spell is cast (1).
Timber Wolves	Summon Wolves	Green	G	1/1	Bands
Titania's Song	Enchantment	Green	3G	--	All artifacts lose their abilities and become artifact creatures with power/toughness=casting cost. When Titania's Song leaves play, artifacts are returned to normal before untap of next turn.
Tranquility	Sorcery	Green	2G	--	Destroys all enchantments.
Tropical Island	Land	Beige	--	--	Tap for 1 blue or green mana.
Tsunami	Sorcery	Green	3G	--	Destroys all islands.
Tundra	Land	Beige	--	--	Tap for 1 blue or white mana.
Tunnel	Instant	Red	R	--	Buries one wall.
U					
Underground Sea	Land	Beige	--	--	Tap for 1 black or blue mana.
Unholy Strength	Enchant Creature	Black	B	--	Gives +2/+1.
Unstable Mutation	Enchant Creature	Blue	U	--	Gives +3/+3; gets -1/-1 token each upkeep; tokens remain even if enchantment is removed.
Unsummon	Instant	Blue	U	--	Return creature to owner's hand.

Appendix H

Card Name	Card Type	Color	Casting Cost	Power/ Toughness	Text
Uthden Troll	Summon Troll	Red	2R	2/2	Regenerates (1).
V					
Verduran Enchantress	Summon Enchantress	Green	1GG	0/2	Can draw a card whenever you cast an enchantment.
Vesuvan Doppelganger	Summon Doppelganger	Blue	3UU	*/*	Where * = copies creature but not color, can change creature imitated during upkeep.
Veteran Bodyguard	Summon Bodyguard	White	2WW	2/5	When not tapped, it takes all damage done to you.
Volcanic Eruption	Sorcery	Blue	XUUU	--	Destroys X mountains in play doing 1 damage to all players and creatures for each destroyed (was X damage).
Volcanic Island	Land	Beige	--	--	Tap for 1 blue or red mana.
W					
Wall of Air	Summon Wall	Blue	1UU	1/5	Flying; wall.
Wall of Bone	Summon Wall	Black	2B	1/4	Wall; regenerates (B).
Wall of Brambles	Summon Wall	Green	2G	2/3	Wall; regenerates (G).
Wall of Fire	Summon Wall	Red	1RR	0/5	Wall; +1/+0 (R).
Wall of Ice	Summon Wall	Green	2G	0/7	Wall
Wall of Stone	Summon Wall	Red	1RR	0/8	Wall
Wall of Swords	Summon Wall	White	3W	3/5	Flying; wall.
Wall of Water	Summon Wall	Blue	1UU	0/5	Wall; +1/+0 (U).
Wall of Wood	Summon Wall	Green	G	0/3	Wall
Wanderlust	Enchant Creature	Green	2G	--	1 damage to creature's controller during upkeep.
War Mammoth	Summon Mammoth	Green	3G	3/3	Trample
Warp Artifact	Enchant Artifact	Black	BB	--	1 damage during upkeep to artifact's controller.
Water Elemental	Summon Elemental	Blue	3UU	5/4	
Weakness	Enchant Creature	Black	B	--	Gives -2/-1.
Web	Enchant Creature	Green	G	--	Gives +0/+2; allows creature to block flying creatures.

Card Name	Card Type	Color	Casting Cost	Power/ Toughness	Text
Wheel of Fortune[1, 3]	Sorcery	Red	2R	--	All discard and draw a new hand.
White Knight	Summon Knight	White	WW	2/2	First strike; protection from black.
White Ward	Enchant Creature	White	W	--	Gives protection from white.
Wild Growth	Enchant Land	Green	G	--	+1 green mana to any land when tapped for mana (was whenever tapped).
Will-O-The-Wisp	Summon Will-O-The-Wisp	Black	B	0/1	Flying; regenerates (B).
Winter Orb	Artifact	Brown	2	--	All players untap only one land per turn.
Wooden Sphere	Artifact	Brown	1	--	+1 life when green spell cast (1).
Wrath of God	Sorcery	White	2WW	--	All creatures in play are destroyed and cannot regenerate.
Z					
Zombie Master	Summon Lord	Black	1BB	2/3	All Zombies get swampwalk and regeneration.

Index

Also available from Wordware Publishing, Inc.

Deep Magic™:
Advanced Strategies for Experienced Players of Magic: The Gathering™
by Charles Wolfe and George H. Baxter

Foreword by Zak Dolan, World Champion Magic player

280 pages • 6 x 9
ISBN: 1-55622-461-3 $14.95

and

Mastering Magic™ Cards
by Larry W. Smith, Ph.D. and George H. Baxter

Foreword by Richard Garfield, Creator of Magic Cards

240 pages • 6 x 9
ISBN: 1-55622-457-5 $15.95

For more information or to order, contact:
Wordware Publishing, Inc.
1506 Capital Avenue
Plano, Texas 75074
(214) 423-0090